AIR CAMPAIGN

WINTER WAR 1939–40

Repelling the Soviets from Finnish skies

KARI STENMAN | ILLUSTRATED BY ADAM TOOBY

OSPREY PUBLISHING
Bloomsbury Publishing Plc
Kemp House, Chawley Park, Cumnor Hill, Oxford OX2 9PH, UK
Bloomsbury Publishing Ireland Limited,
29 Earlsfort Terrace, Dublin 2, D02 AY28, Ireland
1359 Broadway, 12th Floor, New York, NY 10018, USA
E-mail: info@ospreypublishing.com
www.ospreypublishing.com

OSPREY is a trademark of Osprey Publishing Ltd

First published in Great Britain in 2026

A catalogue record for this book is available from the British Library.

ISBN: PB 9781472870575; eBook 9781472870568; ePDF 9781472870599;
XML 9781472870582

26 27 28 29 30   10 9 8 7 6 5 4 3 2 1

Maps and diagrams by www.bounford.com
3D BEVs by Paul Kime
Index by Alison Worthington
Typeset by Lumina Datamatics Ltd
Printed by Repro India Ltd.

Title page: see caption on p. 89.

Osprey Publishing supports the Woodland Trust, the UK's leading woodland conservation
charity.

To find out more about our authors and books visit www.ospreypublishing.com. Here
you will find extracts, author interviews, details of forthcoming events and the option to
sign up for our newsletter.

For product safety-related questions contact productsafety@bloomsbury.com

Photos
All photos not otherwise credited are
courtesy of the author's collection.

Born in 1945, Kari Stenman studied
economics and was an import-export
specialist until Finland's EU accession
in 1995, when he turned his hobby of
aviation history into a profession,
founding a company to publish his
research. He retired in 2009 but has
continued to research and write about the
Finnish air force. In over 50 years in this
field, he has written more than 100 titles.

CONTENTS

INTRODUCTION

The best Finnish fighter in the mid-1930s was the English Bristol Bulldog. Here, Bulldog IVAs of LLv 26 are shown at Academic Air Defence Association courses at Helsinki Malmi on 11 July 1939. The closest machines are serialled BU-62 and BU-66. At the outbreak of the Winter War, there were still ten serviceable Bulldogs on duty. Though already obsolete, the Bulldogs would still score four air victories in the Winter War.

As the mid-1930s approached and the international situation deteriorated, Finland reconsidered its defence requirements. The needs of the Finnish Air Force's trainer aircraft had, for many years, been solved by the construction, under licence, of Czechoslovak Letov S 218 Smolik aircraft. In addition, the multi-role trainer Tuisku, developed by the State Aircraft Factory, was reaching series production. However, equipment in all six Finnish air stations was becoming obsolete.

In the reconnaissance squadrons, Lentolaivue 12 (LLv 12) had just received new Dutch Fokker C.V aircraft, but LLv 10 was flying with obsolete Czechoslovak Aero A.32 planes. In the fighter squadrons, LLv 24 had flown British Gloster Gamecocks since the end of 1929 and began to need a new type. At the beginning of 1935, LLv 26 had just been equipped with new English Bristol Bulldogs. But, technical developments were progressing rapidly, with other European countries shifting to all-metal, low-wing monoplanes with retractable landing gear.

The long-distance and bomber squadron, LLv 44, was equipped with Junkers K.43 aircraft in 1931 but was soon in need of more modern planes. Meanwhile, the maritime squadrons had obsolete English Blackburn Ripon biplanes, and domestic-built VL Kotkas and Sääskis.

The modernization of the Finnish Air Force was accelerated in 1936, when a five-year acquisition plan was initiated. The aircraft type in each air command was limited to one.

The Dutch Fokker C.X was chosen for army co-operation tasks, for which two squadrons would be required. Fokker would also supply the fighter command with their D.XXI, at first for two squadrons. Favourable price and licence production rights were the determining factors. The choice of bomber was the British Bristol Blenheim, for two squadrons, along with a manufacturing licence to equip another squadron.

Fixed air stations were moved to mobile air regiments on 1 January 1938. The five-year plans were sound, but severely restricted by limited funds. Time was not in Finland's favour as, by the outbreak of war, only the fighter command was equipped according to plan.

OPPOSITE FINNISH BASES OF THE WINTER WAR

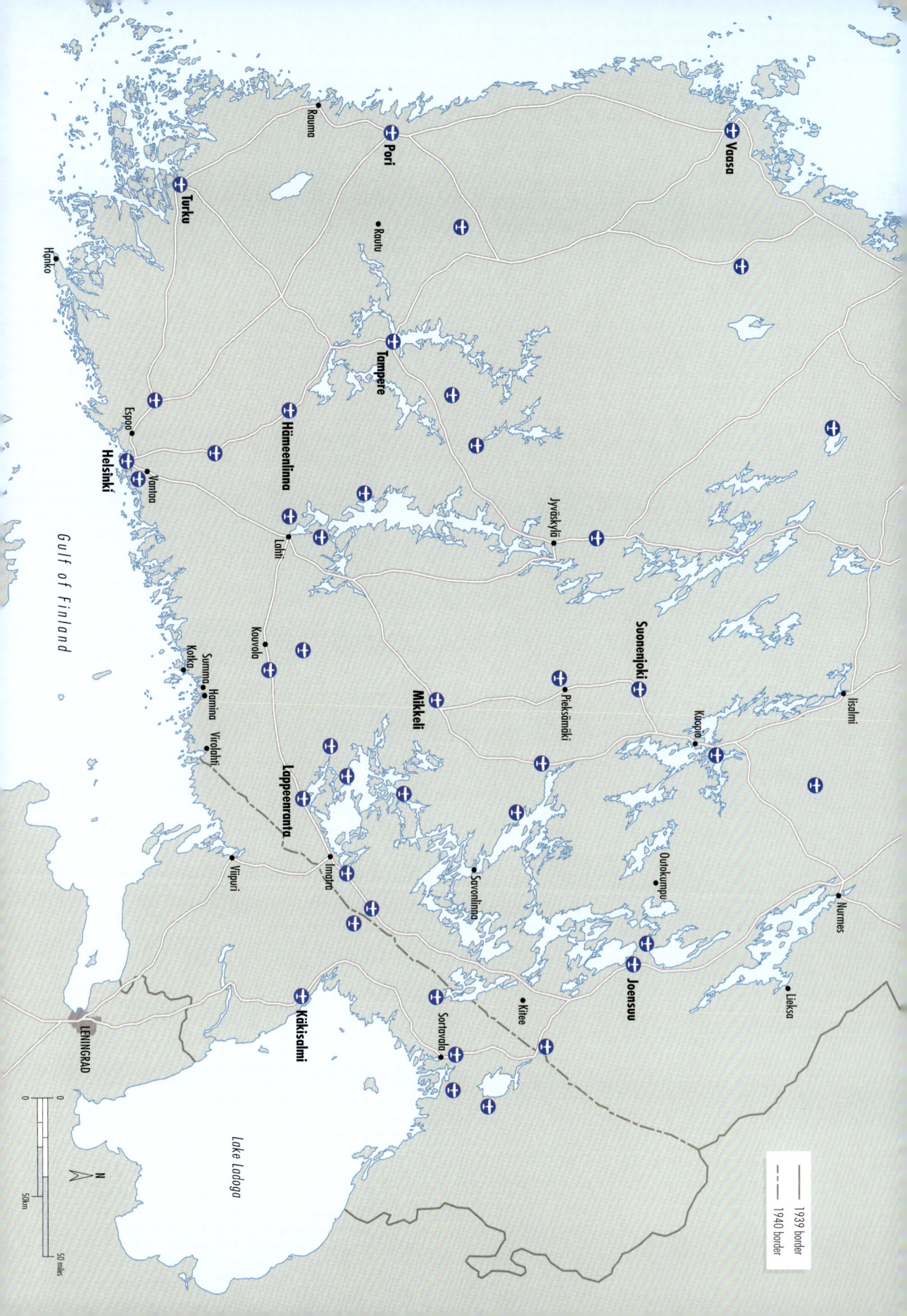

Gulf of Finland

Lake Ladoga

LENINGRAD

Rauma

Pori

Vaasa

Turku

Hanko

Rautu

Espoo

Helsinki

Vantaa

Tampere

Hämeenlinna

Jyväskylä

Lahti

Suonenjoki

Iisalmi

Kuopio

Kouvola

Mikkeli

Pieksämäki

 Outokumpu

Summa

Hamina

Kotka

Virolahti

Nurmes

Lappeenranta

Savonlinna

Lieksa

Viipuri

Imatra

Joensuu

Kitee

Käkisalmi

Sortavala

0

50km

50 miles

N

1939 border
1940 border

CHRONOLOGY

1939

23 August The Ribbentrop-Molotov pact is signed. The secret appendix divides Poland and gives the Soviet Union a free hand over the Baltic countries and Finland.

1 September The Second World War begins with the German invasion of Poland.

5 October The Soviet Union begins its demands to Finland to hand over land and bases.

6 October Finnish mobilization begins.

28 November The Soviet Union cancels its non-aggression pact with Finland.

30 November The Soviet offensive begins, starting the Winter War.

1 December Finnish fighters shoot down 13 Soviet bombers.

19 December Finnish fighters shoot down 11 bombers.

23 December Finnish fighters shoot down seven bombers and five fighters.

25 December The Finnish Army has halted Soviet advances in all directions.

1940

12 January Swedish voluntary unit, F 19, begins operations in Lapland.

17 January Finnish fighters shoot down ten bombers.

19 January Dive bombers of Finland's LLv 10 cause havoc among Russian troops crammed at Pitkäranta.

20 January LLv 44 successfully bombs a large Soviet air base on the frozen Karkunlampi lake.

29 January Dive bombers of LLv 10 sink two large Soviet ships at Saunasaari pier by Lake Ladoga.

1 February After regrouping the Red Army begins a new offensive on the Karelian Isthmus.

11 February The Red Army forces the Finns to retreat on the Karelian Isthmus.

26 February LLv 46 bombs Lotinanpelto air base at River Svir, Russia, with all its available Blenheims.

29 February Soviet fighters shoot down six Finnish fighters during take-off and the ensuing combat at Ruokolahti.

3 March The Soviets begin the crossing of the frozen Viipurinlahti to the rear of the Finnish defences.

8 March Peace negotiations start at Moscow.

11 March At Viipurinlahti the Soviets are beaten and the front remains in Finnish possession.

13 March Winter War ends at 1100hrs Finnish time, with the Moscow Peace Treaty.

This Tupolev SB (2M-100) bomber '9' of 41 SBAP was shot down by 1Lt Jussi Räty, flying Fokker FR-115 of 4/LLv 24 on 1 December 1939, and bellied at Imatra. Here, the evacuation has started. The airframe was transported to the State Aircraft Factory located at Tampere. In all, the factory refurbished eight SB bombers, which were captured during the Winter War for the Finnish Air Force. (SA-kuva)

ATTACKER'S CAPABILITIES

Soviet air forces

During the autumn of 1939, the Russians had concentrated their troops on the Karelian Isthmus (7th Army), and in the areas of Aunus-Porajärvi (8th Army), Repola-Uhtua-Kantalahti (9th Army) and Petsamo (14th army). On the 1,000-mile-long border were half a million men in well over 20 divisions, which were supported by 2,000 pieces of artillery, 2,000 armoured vehicles and over 2,000 aircraft. The number of men would double during the course of the conflict. The number of cannons, tanks and aircraft would each also increase by a thousand.

On 30 November 1939, the order of battle of the Soviet regular and naval air forces on the Finnish front was as follows.

7th Army air forces

The 7th Army air forces were led by Maj. Gen. S.G. Korjunov, and comprised:

15 SBAB, Col. I.G. Pyatyhin, with HQ at Gorelovo
- 2 SBAP, Col. B.P. Pisarsky, at Soltshy and Ropsha with 63 SB
- 24 SBAP, Maj. G.I. Belitsky, at Vitino with 57 SB
- 41 SBAP, Col. I. Ye. Kolomiyech, at Gorelovo with 49 SB

16 SBAB, Col. N.G. Belov, with HQ at Chernevo
- 13 SBAP, Col. S.F. Ushakov, at Chernevo with 53 SB
- 54 SBAP, Col. V.S. Leonov, at Smuryayevo with 51 SB

55 SBAB, Col. N.F. Naumenko, with HQ at Staraya Russa
- 44 SBAP, Col. N.I. Dmitriyev, at Krasnogvadeysk and Zaychevo with 47 SB
- 58 SBAP, Col. I.D. Odonin, at Staraya Russa and Sivotsy with 48 SB

Polikarpov I-15bis fighter '173' was captured intact on the ice of Oulunjärvi, where this 19 IAP machine made a forced landing on 24 December 1939. The State Aircraft Factory refurbished the fighter, and it served in the Finnish Air Force with serial VH-11. The factory repaired another four captured I-15bis fighters for the Finnish Air Force, which served later as advanced trainers.

OPPOSITE SOVIET BASES OF THE WINTER WAR

59 IAB, Col. Ye.Ye. Yerlykin, with HQ at Levashovo
- 7 IAP, Maj. Ye.G. Turenko, at Levashovo and Kasimovo with 33 I-15 bis and 35 I-16
- 25 IAP, Maj. N.S. Toroptshin, at Pushkin with 11 I-15 bis and 34 I-16
- 38 IAP, Maj. N.T. Syusyukalov, at Pushkin with 49 I-15bis, 30 I-153 and 53 I-16
- 68 IAP, Maj. V.V. Zelenchov, at Pushkin and Lempaala with 15 I-153 and 53 I-16

Detached
- 3 LBAP, Maj. P.V. Novikov, at Krasnogvadeysk with 43 R-5
- 9 SBAP, Col. Valkov, at Yedrovo, Kretsy and Krechevichy with 63 I-15bis
- 10 SBAP, Col. G.I. Shuvilov, at Krasnogvadeysk with 42 SB
- 35 SBAP, Maj. G.A. Suhorebnikov, at Siverskaya with 62 SB
- 50 SBAP, Maj. V.V. Smirnov, at Razliv and Siverskaya with 56 SB
- 1 DRAE, at Krechevichy and Gorelovo with 14 SB
- 9 KAO, at Korostovichy with 6 R-5
- 16 KAO, at Korostovichy with 7 SSS

The 7th Army air forces were tasked with bombardment of air bases, military installations, the arms industry, rail and road junctions and stations up to Tampere in the west and Kuopio in the north, and – more importantly – with the direct support of the troops attacking on the Karelian Isthmus, which linked the Leningrad area of Russia with southern Finland, home to the capital Helsinki.

8th Army air forces
The 8th Army air forces were led by Maj. Gen. I.I. Kopets, and comprised:

14 AB, Col. Ye.Ya. Holzakov, at Krestsy
- 49 IAP, Maj. M.A. Bugayev, at Nurmoila and Lodeinoje with 38 I-15bis and 34 I-16
- Part of 72 SBAP, Col. G.A. Shanin, at Besovech and Nurmoila with 30 I-15 bis and 23 SB

Ilyushin DB-3 bomber '14' was also shot down by fighters on the first combat mission of 42 DBAP. The plane came down in the forest at Läskelä, north of Lake Ladoga on 3 February 1940. Again, the airframe was taken to the aircraft factory for inspection. A total of five DB-3 bombers captured during the Winter War were refurbished by the State Aircraft Factory. (SA-kuva)

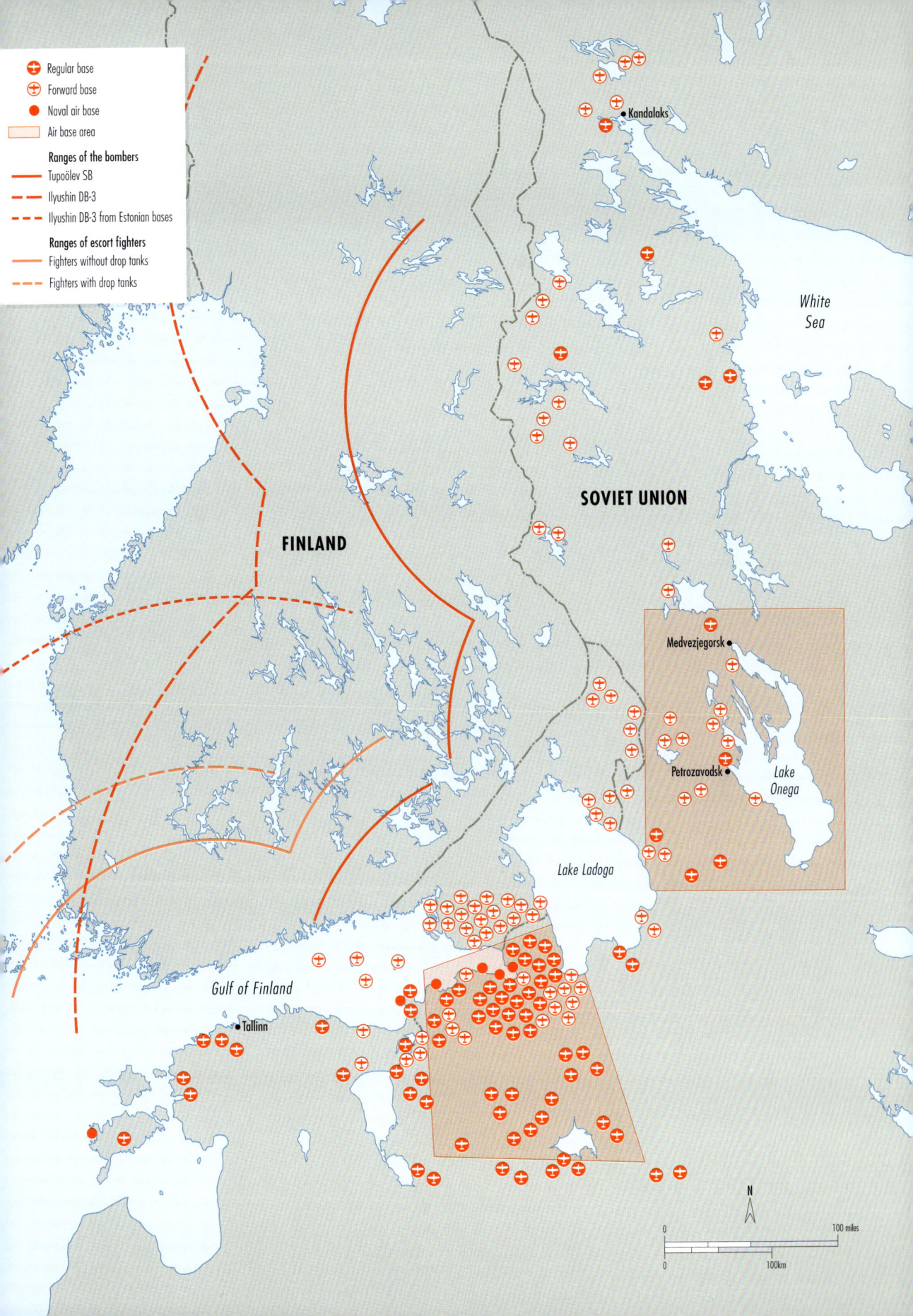

Regular base
Forward base
Naval air base
Air base area

Ranges of the bombers
Tupoõlev SB
Ilyushin DB-3
Ilyushin DB-3 from Estonian bases

Ranges of escort fighters
Fighters without drop tanks
Fighters with drop tanks

Kandalaks

*White
Sea*

SOVIET UNION

FINLAND

Medvezjegorsk

Petrozavodsk

*Lake
Onega*

Lake Ladoga

Gulf of Finland

Tallinn

N

0   100 miles

0
100km

The 8th Army air forces were tasked with bombardment of traffic junctions and air bases, as well as reconnaissance, artillery fire control, and transport and supply missions.

9th Army air forces
The 9th Army air forces were led by CO P.V. Rychakov, and comprised:
- Part of 72 SBAP, Capt. A.I. Zafronov, at Uhtua with 14 I-15bis

The early main task of the 9th Army air forces was the bombardment of the Lapland traffic connections level with Oulu in the west.

14th Army air forces
The 14th Army air forces were led by CO S.A. Krasovsky, and comprised:
- 5 OSAP, Maj. N.G. Sebryakov, at Murmashi and Shongui with 44 I-15bis, 18 I-16 and 24 SB
- DB escadrille, at Murmashi and Vaenga with 23 DB-3

The task of the 14th Army air forces was to defend Murmansk and the Arctic Sea coasts, not only from the Finnish forces, but – critically – from a probable Allied invasion.

Baltic Fleet air forces
The Baltic Fleet air forces were led by Maj. Gen. V.V. Yermachenkov, and comprised:

61 IAB, Col. A.M. Morozov, with HQ at Novoyi Petergof
- 5 IAP, Maj. A.Z. Dushin, at Nizino with 39 I-16
- 13 IAP, Maj. I.G. Romanenko, at Kotly with 42 I-16
- Special Group, at Bezzabotnoye with 30 I-15bis/I-153
- 11 OIAE, at Kummolovo with 7 I-15bis and 16 I-16
- 12 OIAE, at Lipovo with 30 I-15bis/I-16
- 13 OIAE, at Kuplya with 34 I-15bis/I-16

8 BAB, Col. A.N. Suhanov, with HQ at Kotly
- 1 AP, Col. V.P. Vorobyev, at Bezzabotnoye with 48 DB-3
- Part of 57 AP, Maj S.I. Snetkov, at Kotly with 23 SB

This Tupolev TB-3 heavy bomber '4' of 3 TBAP made a forced landing on the ice of Saunajärvi, near Kuhmo. The damage was light, but the plane was left there and photographed on 14 March 1940, just a day after the Winter War ended. The Gladiators of the Swedish volunteer unit F 19 shot down one of these aircraft in Lapland. (SA-kuva)

10 AB, Maj. Gen. N.T. Petruhin, with HQ at Paldiski
- 12 AE, at Paldiski and Kihelkonna with 17 MBR-2
- 43 AE, at Gori Valdai with 12 MBR-2
- 44 AE, at Paldiski with 12 MBR-2
- Part of 57 AP, at Kotly with 25 SB
- Fighter Group, at Paldiski with 9 I-15bis and 3 I-153

15 MRAP, Lt Col. D.F. Bartnovsky, with HQ at Kerstovo
- 6 escadrilles at several bases with 56 MBR-2

LVF (Ladoga Flying Detachment)
- 41 AE, Capt. S.I Kobylskih, at Novaya Ladoga with 11 MBR-2 and 6 SB

The Baltic Fleet air forces were tasked with holding the embargo declared by the Soviet supreme command. This included the bombardment of commercial ports, naval bases and vessels and, especially, preventing the sea traffic to and from neutral Sweden. The numbers of aircraft below denote serviceable planes.

The summary was as follows (split by type and subordination):

Aircraft	7th Army	8th Army	9th Army	14th Army	Baltic Fleet	Total
SB	543	31	–	24	51	649
DB-3	–	–	–	–	53	53
TB-3	–	–	–	74	–	74
I-15bis	157	38	14	44	88	341
I-153	60	–	–	–	22	82
I-16	176	34	–	18	129	357
Others	57	–	–	–	136	193
Total	993	103	14	160	479	1,749

In addition, 219 fighters of Leningrad VO (Air Defence) and 266 bombers of AON-1 (Army for Special Purposes) were available, should they be needed. With these aircraft included, the Soviet Union had concentrated a total of 2,234 combat planes against Finland. By the end of the Winter War this figure had escalated to 3,218. This huge air armada would fly an average of 1,000 sorties per day.

The Soviet bombers were given the task of attacking Finnish air bases, military installations and industrial targets, ports, railway and road junctions, troops and fortifications. But poor navigational skills and the inaccuracy of aerial bombardment also resulted in the bombing of civilian targets. The fighters were tasked with combat air patrol above the front and immediate rear. After the bombers suffered heavy losses, the fighters were assigned to bomber escort duties.

As a comparison, on the main front at the Karelian Isthmus (7th Army sector), the Finns – while facing ten enemy divisions of infantry – could muster five divisions, 300 pieces of artillery, 20 tanks and 114 serviceable combat aircraft, one third being obsolete.

On paper, there was little that this massive Soviet force could not do against its diminutive opponent. But as will be seen later, there were many serious shortcomings of the Soviet military, the biggest one being underestimating the potential of the Finnish armed forces – not least its air force.

BOTTOM LEFT
This Polikarpov I-16 fighter served with 149 IAP, when it was captured almost intact on the ice outside Kotka, on 2 February 1940, after a clash with Gladiators. The factory refurbished the plane, which got the serial VH-201, and later VH-21. It was the only captured I-16 put into flying condition, and it was sent a year later to Germany for evaluation.

BOTTOM RIGHT
During the Winter War, eight captured Polikarpov I-153 fighters were refurbished by the aircraft factory. The first one flying was this VH-101, which was probably captured on 2 February 1940, following a clash with Gladiators outside Hanko, belonging to 38 IAP. It is photographed at the factory at Tampere in March 1940. The plane had a long service with the Finnish Air Force, under the serials VH-11 and IT-11.

DEFENDER'S CAPABILITIES

The Fokker D.XXI was Finland's main fighter type. Here is FR-105 of 5/LLv 24 at Joroinen in April 1940, shortly after the Winter War. The simplicity in construction and systems gave the Fokker a good serviceability in the most demanding winter conditions. The Fokker was a good interceptor, possessing a better rate of climb than any of its Soviet opponents. The armament of four rifle-calibre machine guns was light; early in the conflict, the lack of armour-piercing bullets left something to be desired.

The Finnish Air Force

Army co-op command

Finland's new aviation regiments were created on 1 January 1938 with the disbandment of the earlier air stations. Lentorykmentti 1 (Aviation Regiment 1) was stationed at Suur-Merijoki. Under the same reorganization programme, all army co-operation squadrons were concentrated into the regiment, i.e. LLv 10, LLv 12, LLv 14 and LLv 16.

The five-year basic acquisition programme drawn up in 1937 was for 11 squadrons: three fighter squadrons with 27 planes; one maritime squadron with 13 planes; three long-distance squadrons with nine planes; and four army co-op squadrons with 17 planes. When hostilities started at the end of November 1939, only two army co-op squadrons were equipped, and a third only partly, with fairly modern aircraft – the Fokker C.Xs, which could also be used as dive-bombers. The other two units flew obsolete machines.

Lentorykmentti 1

The Finnish army co-operation aircraft were all concentrated in Lentorykmentti 1, subordinate to the Commander-in-Chief of the air force, Maj. Gen. J.F. Lundqvist, and the flying units were split around in the mobilization.

Fighter command

In 1937, a five-year development plan was issued, under which new fighter aircraft would need to be optimized as interceptors. It was correctly deduced that any attack on Finland would include the large-scale use of bombers without fighter escort. With the limited funds available, the interceptors had to be procured from sources other than the major European powers, since in the growing international tension they simply refused to sell modern warplanes. For the same reason the aircraft acquisition programme was only halfway through when the hostilities

From 1932 onwards, the commander of the Finnish Air Force was Maj. Gen. Jarl Frithiof Lundqvist. He is seen here at his desk at the headquarters at Helsinki Munkkiniemi during the Winter War. In 1941, he was promoted to Lt Gen. and held the office until 1945. Lundqvist was previously an artillery commander, but he was very skilful in getting the best out of the limited funds allotted for the air arm. (SA-kuva)

began. Regardless, based on the five-year plan, seven Fokker D.XXIs and a manufacturing licence for a further 35 similar aircraft were able to be purchased from Holland.

Fighter tactics

Already in 1934, when commanding Lentolaivue 24 and flying Gloster Gamecocks, Maj. Lorentz discovered that, contrary to the traditional form of a lead aircraft and two wingmen, a pair was much more flexible and suited better to most tactical conditions,

LENTORYKMENTTI 1 ORDER OF BATTLE

(30 November 1939)
Regiment Commander Col. Y. Opas, with HQ at Imatra
Lentolaivue 10
Commander Maj. K. Janarmo, with HQ at Lappeenranta
- 1st Flight, 1Lt A. Pietarinen, at Lappeenranta with 4 Fokker C.X
- 2nd Flight, 1Lt H. Kalaja, at Lappeenranta with 4 Fokker C.X
- 3rd Flight, 1Lt L. Mustonen, at Lappeenranta with 4 Fokker C.X
Lentolaivue 12
Commander Maj. A. Nisonen, with HQ at Suur-Merijoki
- 1st Flight, Capt. A. Maunula, at Suur-Merijoki with 5 Fokker C.X
- 2nd Flight, 1Lt I. Salo, at Suur-Merijoki with 4 Fokker C.X
- 3rd Flight, 1Lt A. Bremer, at Suur-Merijoki with 4 Fokker C.X

Lentolaivue 14
Commander Capt. J. Moilanen, with HQ at Laikko
- 1st Flight, 1Lt M. Eskola, at Käkisalmi with 3 Fokker C.X
- 2nd Flight, 1Lt E. Sario, at Laikko with 1 Fokker C.X and 1 Fokker C.V
- 3rd Flight, 1Lt E. Kerke, at Laikko with 5 Fokker C.V
Lentolaivue 16
Commander Capt. A. Viherto, with HQ at Värtsilä
- 1st Flight, 1Lt R. Rautakoura, at Värtsilä with 4 Ripon
- 2nd Flight, 1Lt P. Hyvönen, at Värtsilä with 3 Ripon
- 3rd Flight, Capt. J. Vatanen, at Sortavala with 5 Junkers
LLv 12 was tasked with reconnoitring on the western Karelian Isthmus, and LLv 14 on the eastern isthmus. LLv 16 operated on the north side of Lake Ladoga, and when the waters froze, its 3rd Flight flew north, to the Kainuu area.

OPPOSITE ATTACKING SOVIET BOMBER FORMATIONS

Fokker C.X army co-op plane of LLv 12 in a dug sand-walled shelter at Raulampi, near Viipuri, on 4 October 1939, just a couple of days before the mobilization. During the Winter War, this squadron flew reconnaissance and nuisance missions, mostly nocturnal as the snow gave sufficient light, on the western Karelian Isthmus, where the main Soviet attack occurred.

and could be increased to a four-aircraft swarm without difficulty. Before assuming the command of Lentolaivue 24, Magnusson paid a number of visits to other air forces, including a three-month tour to JG 132 'Richthofen'. The Germans had also given up the three-plane basic form in favour of the 'finger-four' (a novel formation of four planes whose offset-V shape resembles the tips of the fingers of the right hand). This convinced the Finnish top brass that the basic formations, and newly developed tactics, were fundamentally sound.

Due to the lack of funds, the elementary fighter pilots' flying training was complete, but the advanced training did not go through all possible modes of offence, since it was discovered that usually two, or three at the most, types of attacks against the bombers were enough. These three ways and the associated gunnery were rehearsed throughout, and this training served both the doctrine and economical limits. It was also assumed that, in a conflict, the bomber formations would arrive without a fighter escort, which was true for the first half of the war.

The machine guns were usually set to converge at 150m, but the pilots were trained to hold their fire until 50m. Getting there was somewhat risky but, again at that distance behind the bomber, the fighter had two major advantages: firstly, they were out of the sectors of the defensive fire; and, secondly, they could not miss. What is more, the rifle-calibre machine-gun fire did not cause the bomber to explode dangerously.

The Winter War would show the basic formation of a pair of fighters and its multiples to be effective. This gave a tactical advantage to the Finns, in addition to the fact that the offensive had to be taken, even against the Soviets' numerical superiority. The doctrine needed no changes through all conflicts during World War II.

Crucially, the Finnish pilots were also fighting for their country and existence, which imbued them with a substantive and effective motivation. In addition, the pilots were very well trained and taught to make the best they could of the prevailing conditions.

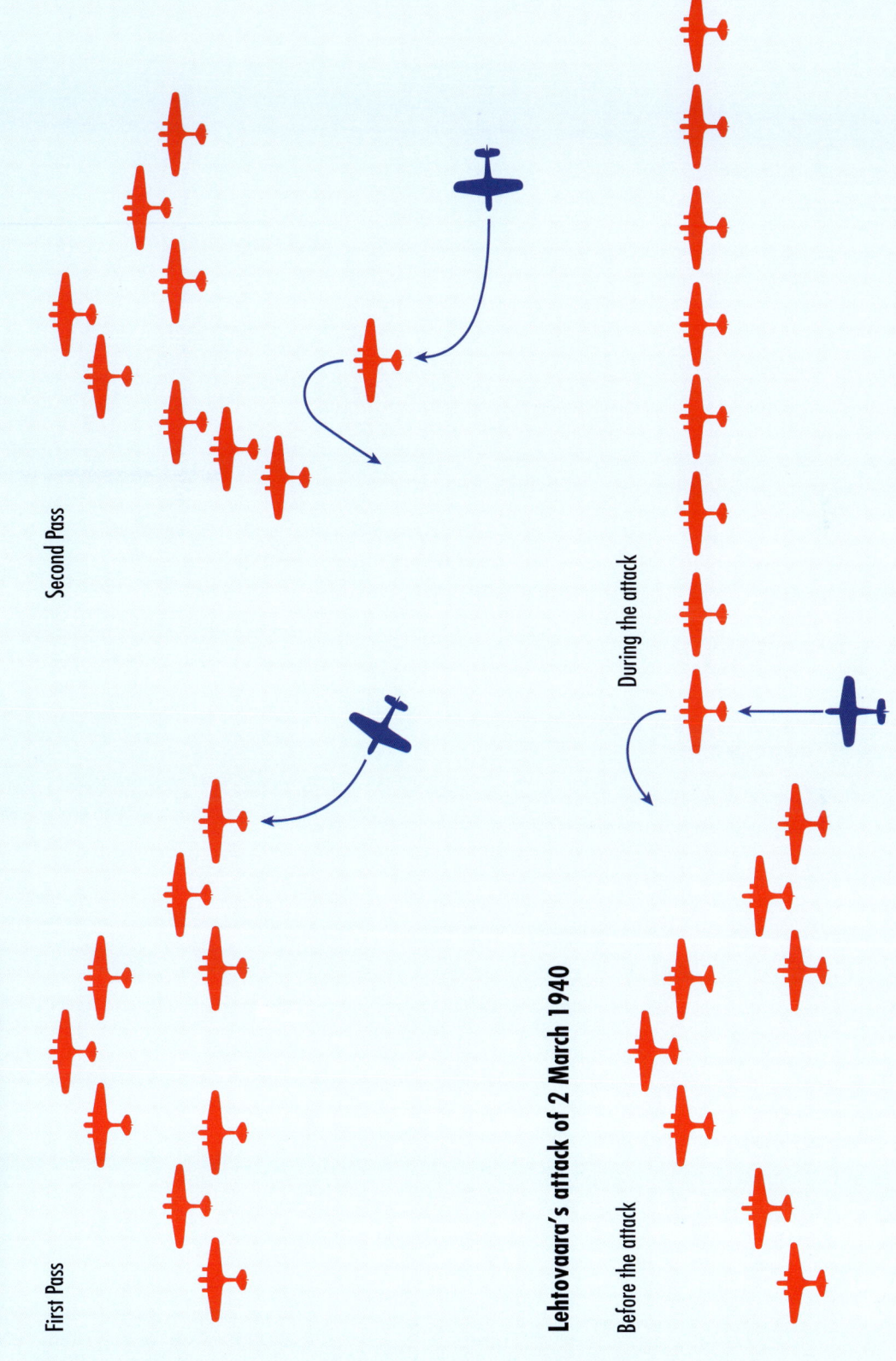

Luukkanen's attack of 6 January 1940

First Pass

Second Pass

Lehtovaara's attack of 2 March 1940

Before the attack

During the attack

Total number of Finnish aircraft at the beginning of the Winter War				
Serial prefix	Type	Role	Origin	Number
FR	Fokker D.XXI	fighter	Netherlands	42
FA	Fiat G.50	fighter	Italy	35
BW	Brewster Model 239	fighter	United States	44
GL	Gloster Gladiator	fighter	Britain (and donated by Sweden)	30
GT	Gloster Gauntlet	fighter	Britain (donated by South Africa)	24
MS	Morane-Saulnier M.S. 406	fighter	France	30
CA	Caudron-Renault C.R. 714	fighter	France	6
BU	Bristol Bulldog	fighter	Britain	19
RO	Blackburn Roc	fighter	Britain	0
HU	Hawker Hurricane	fighter	Britain	12
FK	Fokker C.X	reconnaissance/light bomber	Netherlands	59
FO	Fokker C.VE	reconnaissance	Netherlands	19
	Fokker C.VD	reconnaissance	Netherlands (donated by Sweden)	
BL	Bristol Blenheim	bomber	Britain	42
LY	Westland Lysander	liaison	Britain	12
JF	Jaktfalken	advanced trainer (designed as a fighter, but obsolete)	Sweden	3
KO	Koolhoven F.K. 52	reconnaissance	Netherlands (donated by Count von Rosen)	2
DC	Douglas DC-2	transport	United States (donated by Count von Rosen)	1
FE	Fokker F.VIII	transport	Netherland (donated by Count von Rosen)	1
RI	Blackburn Ripon	maritime	Britain	26
JU	Junkers F13	liaison	Germany	13
	Junkers K.43	transport	Germany	

Lentorykmentti 2

The reorganization of 1 January 1938 transformed the air stations into flexible aviation regiments. Lentoasema 1 at Utti became Lentorykmentti 2, which had Lentolaivue 24 and 26 at its disposal, and thus the first fighter regiment in Finland came to existence.

During the course of 1938 and the first half of 1939, Lentolaivue 24 passed over the obsolete Gamecocks to training units, and all three flights became fully equipped with Fokker D.XXIs. Also, Lentolaivue 26 received – in addition to the ageing Bulldogs – enough Fokkers to equip two flights.

The Finnish fighter defences were all concentrated into Lentorykmentti 2, commanded by Lt Col. Richard Lorentz. He had two fighter squadrons, which during the mobilization he had positioned elsewhere from their usual bases. On 26 November 1939, Fokker D.XXIs and their pilots of Lentolaivue 26 were transferred to sister squadron Lentolaivue 24, mainly forming the 1st and 5th Flights.

Lt Col. Richard Lorentz commanded Lentorykmentti 2 from October 1939 onwards until June 1943. He is shown here as a colonel in his office at Äänislinna in late June 1942. Lorentz was the developer of the tactical formation of a pair and 'finger-four' in 1934, before the Germans, who first tested it in the Spanish Civil War. (SA-kuva)

LENTORYKMENTTI 2 ORDER OF BATTLE

(30 November 1939)
Regiment Commander Lt Col. R. Lorentz, with
HQ at Immola
Lentolaivue 24
Commander Capt. G. Magnusson, with HQ at Immola
1st Flight, Capt. E. Carlsson, at Immola with 6 Fokker D.XXI
2nd Flight, 1Lt J. Vuorela, at Suur-Merijoki with 6 Fokker D.XXI
3rd Flight, 1Lt E. Luukkanen, at Immola with 6 Fokker D.XXI
4th Flight, Capt. G. Magnusson, at Immola with 7 Fokker D.XXI
5th Flight, 1Lt L. Ahola at Immola, with 10 Fokker D.XXI

Lentolaivue 26
Commander Capt. E. Heinilä, with HQ at Heinjoki
Det Heinilä, Capt. E. Heinilä, at Heinjoki with
10 Bulldog
The whole modern fighter force was thus Lentolaivue 24. Its commander Capt. 'Eka' Magnusson was later to show exceptional tactical and personal leadership. The 35 Fokkers in five flights, ready to be spread around southeast Finland, were manned with well-trained and well-motivated pilots, ready to defend their country. The task was to protect the traffic junctions in southeast Finland and prevent Soviet attacks on and through the Karelian Isthmus.

Bomber command

In 1936 the Finnish Air Force became interested in a new modern bomber, the Bristol Blenheim, and 18 aircraft were ordered from Britain. The first two aircraft arrived in July 1937 and the rest followed within a year. During this period a manufacturing licence was obtained from the Bristol Aeroplane Company, and the State Aircraft Factory received an order for 15 bombers in April 1939.

When the air force was reorganized on 1 January 1938, the firm air stations were disbanded and aviation regiments were formed instead. Air Station 6 became Aviation Regiment 4 (LeR 4), operating from new Immola air base. Both long-range squadrons, LLv 44 and 46, were equipped with the Blenheim.

Lt Col. Toivo Somerto commanded Lentorykmentti 4 from October 1939 until April 1942, when he was put into retirement. By training, he was an observer and navigator. Somerto is seen here at his desk at regiment headquarters at Luonetjärvi, early during the Continuation War in July 1941. (SA-kuva)

The five-year plan from 1937 consisted, among others, of three long-range (bomber and reconnaissance) squadrons, each with nine aircraft. When the hostilities broke out in November 1939, only two long-range squadrons were equipped with modern aircraft, since the factory had not even begun the licence production.

Lentorykmentti 4

The Finnish bomber and long-range command was concentrated into LeR 4, reporting to the general HQ and during the mobilization the flying units were transferred to the rear at Luonetjärvi.

LENTORYKMENTTI 4 ORDER OF BATTLE

(30 November 1939)
Regiment Commander Lt Col. T. Somerto, with HQ at Luonetjärvi
Lentolaivue 44
Commander Maj. E. Stenbäck, with HQ at Luonetjärvi
1st Flight, Capt. O. Lumiala, at Luonetjärvi with 2 Blenheims
2nd Flight, 1Lt K. Pirhonen, at Luonetjärvi with 3 Blenheims
3rd Flight, 1Lt B. Ek, at Luonetjärvi with 3 Blenheims

Lentolaivue 46
Commander Maj. O. Sarko, with HQ at Luonetjärvi
1st Flight, Capt. J. Piponius, at Luonetjärvi with 3 Blenheims
2nd Flight, Capt. K. Kepsu, at Luonetjärvi with 3 Blenheims
3rd Flight, 1Lt O. Siirilä, at Luonetjärvi with 3 Blenheims
The regiment was tasked with bombardment and reconnaissance, specified by the supreme command. At the beginning, the regiment was concentrated on areas that lacked other aerial reconnaissance, such as the northeast of Lake Ladoga and northwards along the border to Uhtua.

Maritime command

On 1 January 1938, seaplanes were still equipping three air stations out of six. In the reforms the seaplane stations were disbanded and the third, Lentoasema 2 based at Santahamina near Helsinki, was downgraded to merely a Detached Squadron, with Lt Col. G. von Behr remaining in command. At its establishment, the squadron was equipped with nine Blackburn Ripon floatplanes, which could be fitted with skis or wheels.

In October 1939, Finland began to prepare for a conflict. Large military exercises were held on the Karelian Isthmus and the terrain was fortified. On 10 October the flying part of the Detached Squadron was formed into Lentolaivue 36, commanded by Capt. H. Helenius.

On 30 November 1939, when the Soviet Union attacked Finland, LLv 36 was based at Kallvik, east of Helsinki. Two flights, led by 1Lt J. Gabrielsson and 1Lt L. Karjalainen, altogether had six Ripons (RI) and the unit was tasked with maritime reconnaissance, submarine hunting and local bombardments in the Gulf of Finland. Additionally, T-LLv 39 was subordinated to the squadron, flying Coast Guard Junkers F 13 floatplanes in anti-submarine searches in the Aaland Sea.

Foreign help

Right after the outbreak of World War II, the Finnish purchasing commissions were out for aircraft. Many other nations were also in the same business. Military materiel became more difficult to obtain and prices escalated. Under the threat of the Soviet Union, Finland's position was becoming increasingly alarming and instructions were given to buy any planes that could be acquired.

Italy

The only type immediately available from Europe was the Italian Fiat G.50 fighter. On 23 October 1939, a deal with Fiat was concluded for 25 aircraft. The purchase also included spares and 750,000 rounds of ammunition. This was extended by another batch of ten fighters bought on 14 January 1940.

Finnish serials FA-1 to FA-35 inclusive were given to the fighters. The aircraft were shipped to Sweden for assembly and collected by Finnish pilots. Two aircraft were lost en route, and of the remainder, all but one were in Finland by 12 March 1940. The last plane came on 19 June 1940 and thus 33 of the ordered 35 aircraft had arrived.

Both two and, later, all three Finnish long-range and bomber squadrons were equipped with the Bristol Blenheim. Here is a brand new, long-nose Blenheim IV coded BL-130 of LLv 46, on a visit to Kauhava on 28 January 1940. Bristol painted the bombers according to Finnish instructions. After four weeks of training, the unit commenced missions with their new machines, starting with a full-squadron bombing of Lotinanpelto air base, by the River Svir.

In late 1939, Italy was the only source for modern combat aircraft. Finland bought in two lots of 35 Fiat G.50 fighters. They would have made it to the Winter War, but Germany prevented their transit and only a dozen were in time to see action in the conflict. Here is FA-32 in gun harmonization at Torslanda, Sweden, before the transfer flight to Finland, which took place on 12 March 1940. It was one of seven fitted with the enclosed cockpit.

30 Gloster Gladiator fighters were obtained from England, all of which would see action in the Winter War with Llv 26. In the assembly in Sweden, the planes were fitted with Swedish skis, which remained in Finnish use long afterwards. Here is GL-276 photographed at Utti during the conflict, seeing first service with Llv 26, until delivered on 1 March 1940 to Llv 14. The Gladiators wore the standard British shadow-shade camouflage.

USA

In the USA, purchases had commenced on 17 October 1939, leading to a contract with Brewster Aeronautical Corporation on 16 December 1939 for 44 Brewster Model 239 fighters, with spare parts, ten spare engines and 20 propellers. The fighters were shipped in four consignments to Bergen, Norway and then by rail to Sweden for assembly. The serials were BW-351 to BW-394 inclusive and the fighters were collected by 1 May 1940.

Britain

Immediately after the outbreak of the Winter War, ambassadors in Britain and France authorized by the Finnish government approached the respective governments for any kind of military materiel, especially aircraft, that could be made operational quickly.

In Britain, the Air Ministry had already agreed on 5 December 1939 to supply second-line aircraft to Finland, and the first contract was signed between the Gloster Aircraft Company and the Finnish government a week later. Through this arrangement, the British government was able to avoid any potential political confrontation with the Soviet Union. Similar contracts with Bristol, Westland and Blackburn were to follow.

On 12 December 1939, Finland bought 20 Gloster Gladiator II fighters, and received a further ten free of charge. These fighters were shipped to Bergen, Norway and from there by rail to Sweden for assembly. Finnish crews picked the aircraft up between 18 January and 16 February 1940. The serials for these were GL-251 to GL-280 inclusive.

Twelve Blenheim IVs were bought from Bristol on 24 December 1939. Finnish aircrews picked up the bombers on 17 January 1940 and all but two were in Finland four days later. One was lost over the North Sea and the final one arrived on 5 June 1940. The serials were BL-122 to BL-133.

A total of 17 Westland Lysander Is were released on 8 January 1940. Nine were shipped to Sweden for assembly and three were flown to Sweden, one being lost in Norway. Finnish airmen picked up the planes and flew them to Finland by 3 May 1940. The serials were LY-114 to LY-125.

On 27 January 1940, Finland accepted the offer to purchase 33 Roc Is from Blackburn. The intention was to fly them to Finland in four consignments with four-to-five day intervals. The first four (RO-141 to RO-144) made it to Dyce, Scotland on 13 March 1940. However, the Moscow Peace Treaty on the same day (between the Soviet Union and Finland) halted their delivery, and the aircraft remained in Scotland.

In early February 1940, another 12 Blenheims were released for Finland. These were Mark Is and British crews flew them to Finland, all arriving on 26 February 1940. The serials were BL-134 to BL-145. Then on 17 February 1940, a dozen Hurricane I fighters were bought from Hawker.

Finnish crews collected these in two consignments and flew them to Finland by 10 March 1940. Two aircraft were lost en route and the serials of those received were HU 451 to HU 460.

From the UK, 4 million .303in cartridges were delivered, as well as 2,000 120lb (54kg) GP (general purpose) bombs and 7,000 250lb (113kg) GP bombs, plus 6,000 4lb (1.8kg) incendiaries. Also, 15,000 signal cartridges were sent. Seventeen British technicians had worked in Swedish assembly plants since January 1940, and 24 more were on the way when the war ended.

South Africa

The Federation of South Africa donated 24 Gloster Gauntlet IIs, which were shipped from Great Britain to Sweden by 10 March 1940. Nine aircraft were assembled in Sweden and collected by Finnish crews, taking them to Finland by 12 April 1940. The rest were shipped to Finland, arriving on 17 May 1940. Serials for these were GT-395 to GT-418.

France

France was not as concerned about its political image and their military attaché in Helsinki received a telegram on 28 December 1939 informing them that the French government had initially decided to donate 50 fighters to Finland, in addition to airfield equipment, spares, coolants and 1.35 million rounds of ammunition.

Out of these 50 Morane-Saulnier M.S. 406 fighters, only 30 aircraft were shipped to Sweden for assembly. Finnish serials MS301 to MS330 inclusive were applied. Finnish pilots collected the Moranes. The first two departed to Finland on 4 February 1940 and all were picked up in two to five aircraft consignments by the end of the month. A while later, the list was expanded by 80 Caudron-Renault C.R. 714 and 46 Koolhoven F.K. 58 fighters and 62 Potez 633 bombers.

Concerning the C.R. 714 fighters, the original idea was to first supply a fully-operational squadron with pilots and service crews. But only six aircraft finally arrived by 28 May 1940. The Finnish serials were CA-551 to CA-556.

Shortly after the Winter War, Prime Minister Edouard Daladier informed the French parliament that France had donated 145 aircraft and plenty of other military supplies to Finland. Actually, only 30 Moranes and six Caudrons were ever delivered, the latter being totally unsuitable in Finnish conditions.

30 Morane-Saulnier MS.406s were also received as a gift from France. They all arrived during February 1940, just in time to participate in the Winter War. The wheel landing gear caused several flip-overs in landing on the snow. Here is MS307 of 2/LLv 28 at Säkylä in February 1940. The national insignias are still darkened after crossing Sweden. In the centre is the flight leader, 1Lt Reino Turkki, who two decades later became the Finnish Air Force commander.

OPPOSITE SOVIET BOMBARDMENT OF FINLAND

Assembly facilities

At first, the deliveries were made by sea via Sweden, where assembly facilities were organized into four locations:

- AB Aerotransport at Bulltofta, near Malmö
- Centrala Flygverkstaden at Malmslätt, near Malmö
- Götaverken at Torslanda, near Gothenburg
- SAAB at Trollhättan, near Gothenburg

One of the Swedish contributions was sending a flying unit, Flygflottilj 19, to protect Lapland. Here is one of 12 Gladiators, coded 'H', seen at Kauhava on 30 March 1940, on the way back to Sweden. After the conflict, the Finnish national insignias were covered with military honour emblems. By splitting the planes around to forward bases in Lapland, the Swedes gave the impression that they existed everywhere, making the Russian aircrews cautious.

These plants put together 157 aircraft from December 1939 to April 1940.

As the Soviet invasion did not conquer Finland as planned, the Winter War kept on going, and so did expenditure on war materiel. To speed up deliveries of released aircraft, an air route was opened. The shortest way to Finland was from Scotland across the North Sea to the Stavanger area in Norway. From there it passed south of Oslo, across Sweden via Västerås, and finally over the Baltic Sea to southwestern Finland. All this was just over 1,000 miles (1,600km).

The Norwegian government approved the establishment of a small servicing and refuelling point at Stavanger's Sola airfield, where all the aircraft from the UK were to arrive. In Sweden refuelling points were arranged at Västerås, Bromma and Barkarby.

In addition to the 157 aircraft assembled in Sweden, there were 34 more in transit when the war ended, plus plans for another 137 (80 Caudron 714s, 33 Blackburn Rocs, 18 Potez 633s and eight Bristol Blenheims) already released and with transit commenced, but interrupted by the Winter War peace treaty.

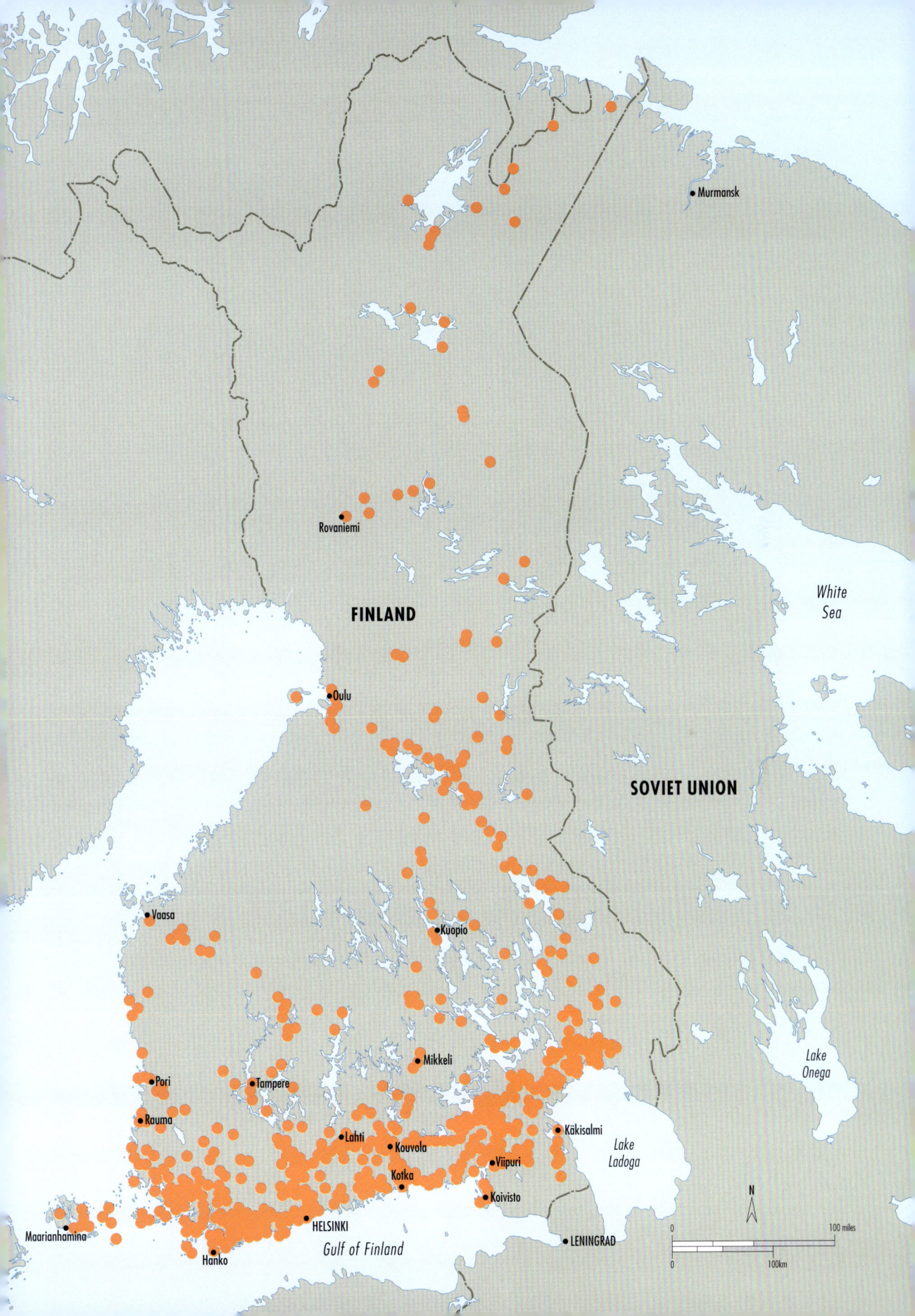

FINLAND

SOVIET UNION

White
Sea

Lake
Onega

Lake
Ladoga

• Murmansk

Rovaniemi

• Oulu

• Vaasa

• Kuopio

• Pori
• Tampere

• Rauma

• Mikkeli

• Lahti

• Kouvola

Kotka

• Käkisalmi

• Viipuri

• Koivisto

Maarianhamina

HELSINKI
Gulf of Finland

Hanko

• LENINGRAD

N

0   100 miles

0   100km

1/LLv 26 (1st Flight of Lentolaivue 26) Bulldog pilots still at peace on 12 August 1939 at Suur-Merijoki air base, west of Viipuri (Vyborg). From left: 2Lt Aarne Alitalo, 2Lt Tapani Harmaja, flight leader Capt. Erkki Heinilä, Sgt Valio Porvari, 1Lt Paavo Berg and MSgt Jussi Tolkki. All these men would participate in the Winter War, which was only three and a half months away.

Swedish support

At the outbreak of the Winter War, the Finnish government asked for immediate help from its closest neighbour, Sweden. They were not much better equipped than Finland, but still acted swiftly and, on 8 December 1939, a decision was made to donate eight older aircraft from the Royal Swedish Air Force stocks.

Two obsolete Bristol Bulldog IIAs and three Jaktfalken fighters, one J 6A and two J 6Bs, were received on 15 December 1939. The former got Finnish serials BUj-214 and 216, based on their previous Swedish serials[1]. Likewise, the Jaktfalkens became JF-219, 224 and 228. On 23 December 1939, three also-obsolete Fokker C.VD reconnaissance aircraft were flown to Finland and serialled FO-19, 23 and 80.

The Gladiators from Britain were not the only Gladiators flying on the Finnish side against the Soviet Union – a dozen Swedish Gladiator Is (or J8s, as they were known in Sweden) were flown to northern Finland on 12 January 1940, and operated quite effectively in the defence of Lapland.

This Swedish volunteer unit Flygflottilj 19 also possessed four Hawker Hart light bombers. For liaison duties it had one Junkers F13 (Finnish civil registration OH-SUO), Waco ZQC-6 (OH-SLA) and Tigerschwalbe RK 26 aircraft. The Gladiators claimed eight Soviet bombers shot down. The Finnish government replaced the losses of six aircraft to the Swedes. All but one aircraft returned to Sweden by 1 April 1940. The Junkers was donated to the Finnish Air Force and became JU-120.

On the civil side, Count Carl Gustaf von Rosen, son of Eric von Rosen of 1918 fame and Swedish aviation pioneer, obtained four aircraft and donated them to the Finnish Air Force. The most useful was a Douglas DC-2 (SE-AKE), which arrived at the end of January 1940, converted to a bomber and serialled DC-1.

On 18 January 1940, two Dutch Koolhoven F.K. 52 reconnaissance aircraft (PH-ASX and ASW) were flown to Finland and given codes KO-129 and 130. Finally, one Fokker F.VIII transport (SE-AHA) was obtained, but could not be flown to Finland until 12 November 1940. It became later FE-1.

---

1   The BUj abbreviation referred to the Jupiter engines of these older Bulldogs, to distinguish them from the later Mercury-powered versions.

CAMPAIGN OBJECTIVES

In spite of the tensions in the international situation, Finland had an exceptionally warm summer of 1939 and everything was peaceful, although volunteers were building light fortifications on the Karelian Isthmus, as a token of defensive will. Finnish politicians did not speak about the possibility of a war, since Finland and the Soviet Union had a non-aggression pact.

One who saw the danger towards Finland was Marshal Carl Gustav Mannerheim. He believed that a major war would break out in Europe and said that some kind of an understanding was evolving between Hitler's Germany and Stalin's Soviet Union, which would be the worst possible scenario for Finland. He did demand more appropriations for Finland's defences, but the politicians knocked out Mannerheim's proposals on the mistaken belief that they were exaggerated.

For almost two years, the Finnish government had – appealing to Finland's neutrality – rejected Soviet proposals for secret security co-operation, and demands for the use of its outer islands in the Gulf of Finland.

Tension in Europe grew when Adolf Hitler, who took power in Germany in early 1933, was not satisfied with the revisions and territorial returns of the Treaty of Versailles after World War I. In March 1938, Hitler annexed Austria to Germany. This was followed by the German-speaking areas (*Sudetenland*) of Czechoslovakia, to which Britain and France agreed upon in the conference held at Munich in September 1938. In March 1939, the rest of Czechoslovakia was annexed to Germany as a protectorate and Lithuania was forced to give up the Memel area. The Soviet Union was trying to build up a coalition against Germany, but the West remained passive.

Next, Hitler demanded the old German city of Danzig, which had been determined as a free city by the Versailles peace treaty. Poland dismissed this categorically. Now, the British and French attitudes changed. They announced that if the independence of Poland was threatened, they would deal with the situation with arms. They tried to negotiate with the Soviet Union for co-operation to help Poland. The negotiations were extended because Britain did not accept Stalin's demand of getting free hands to deal with its neighbours, including Finland.

The mobilization began in Finland on 6 October 1939. Among other things, those aircraft still without a camouflage were hastily given one, including the national insignias. Here is a Blackburn Ripon IIF coded RI-153 of Llv 36, moored at Kallvik east of Helsinki, on 3 November 1939. This unit was used on maritime operations and, especially, submarine search.

Flygflottilj 19 arrived also with four Hawker Hart light bombers, which were mostly used in nocturnal harassment operations on enemy troops. But on their first mission, on 12 January, two Harts collided mid-air and a third was shot down by fighters. Later, one more Hart arrived from Sweden. Here is machine 'M' in flight over Märkäjärvi, Lapland on the way back to Sweden, on 26 March 1940.

Hitler saw now that his opportunity had come. He proposed to the Soviet leader, Joseph Stalin, a non-aggression pact. On 23 August 1939, foreign ministers Joachim von Ribbentrop and Vyacheslav Molotov signed the treaty (known as the Ribbentrop-Molotov pact). In its secret appendix, Poland was divided and the Soviet Union got a free hand to deal with the eastern parts of Romania, the Baltic countries of Estonia and Latvia, plus, a little later, Lithuania and finally, Finland. The worst scenario proposed by Mannerheim had come true.

Germany attacked Poland on 1 September 1939. Two days later, Britain and France declared war on Germany. The Second World War had begun. Germany crushed Poland in three weeks. The Soviet Union occupied the eastern parts of Poland and immediately forced the Baltic countries into delivery of military bases. Finland was invited on 5 October to Moscow for negotiations. The 1920 Tarto peace negotiator, Juho Kusti Paasikivi and his staff was sent. Thousands of people escorted the negotiators at Helsinki main railway station, singing patriotic songs and hymns.

In Moscow the negotiators were received by Stalin and Molotov. On the grounds of maintaining the safety of Leningrad, Stalin demanded areas on the Karelian Isthmus, outer islands in the Gulf of Finland and a military base at Hanko. In return, the Soviet Union offered wide areas of land in Eastern Karelia.

The Finnish negotiators were not authorized to make concessions and they returned to Helsinki for instructions. The government could have accepted the handover of the outer islands in the Gulf of Finland, as well as moving the border slightly on the Karelian Isthmus, but it unanimously rejected renting Hanko for a base. They saw this as impossible for a sovereign and independent country. Finland wanted to remain as an independent western democracy. It relied on the support of the League of Nations and for the military support of Britain, the United States and Sweden.

A day after the invitation to Moscow, an order for mobilization was given under the cover of additional exercises, and Mannerheim was appointed as the supreme commander of the defence forces. The evacuation of the population near the border to inner parts of Finland also commenced. The schools were also closed.

Though the second half of the 1930s saw an economic boom in Finland, the funds for defence were stingy. The politicians believed that the country could stay outside a possible major European war and approached Sweden for co-operation. The negotiators Paasikivi and Väinö Tanner made another two journeys to Moscow, but the negotiations broke down over the Hanko base, which Stalin firmly insisted upon. Molotov's radio speech at the end of October, when he made Stalin's central goals public, showed that a major power does not bargain with its claims.

The Finnish government was pleased with the firm attitude in the negotiations. They did not consider that the end of negotiations would be fatal. Feelings became relaxed and people began returning to their homes near the border. But the crisis was not over. Stalin had earlier received reports from his intelligence service that the Red Army would not face any strong opposition in Finland. The workers and peasants would soon join the Red Army. These reports supported his decision to move from limited goals to conquering the whole country.

The attack was camouflaged as a rescue mission to save the Finnish nation from its oppressors. Otto Ville Kuusinen, who had escaped to Russia in 1918, was authorized by Stalin to form a people's government of Finland. The Soviet Union signed diplomatic relations and a friendship pact with this puppet government (Terijoki government). The establishment of a Kuusinen government showed that the independence of Finland was about to be taken. Stalin's schedule was to ratify the agreement with Kuusinen's government at Helsinki on the former's birthday on 18 December.

To push the blame for starting the war onto the Finns, the Soviets claimed that the Finnish artillery had on 26 November shot at a Mainila village on the Karelian Isthmus, killing four Soviet soldiers. Finland tried to defend itself by stating that the closest artillery batteries were 40km from Mainila and they could not shoot that far. These shots were fired by the Russians themselves. The Soviet Union called off the non-aggression pact on 28 November and broke off diplomatic relations a day later. The Soviet Union then attacked Finland on 30 November 1939.

Finland tried to reinstate the peace by changing the government and asking Sweden to mediate. But the Soviet Union informed Finland that it recognized only the Terijoki government. The Winter War had begun.

As a result of the attack, the League of Nations expelled the Soviet Union and advised all states in the world to help Finland in all possible ways. Strong citizens' reactions forced the politicians into action. Britain and France were planning to send an expeditionary force to Finland. Finland received a lot of sympathy but had to fight alone.

At the outbreak of the war, the strength of the Finnish Army was 295,000 men. There were enough rifles for all, but automatic weapons consisted of only one-third of the need. Cannons, aircraft, anti-tank and anti-aircraft weapons were all too few. The small number of tanks (mostly obsolete) and artillery ammunition were in desperate demand. The equipment

The guilty ones for the Winter War. Signing of the Ribbentrop-Molotov non-aggression pact at Moscow on 23 August 1939. The secret appendix contained the dividing of Poland between Germany and the Soviet Union, and gave the Soviet Union free hands concerning the Baltic countries and Finland. Russian Foreign Minister, Vyacheslav Molotov signs; behind him stands the German Foreign Minister, Joachim von Ribbentrop, and to the left of him, the Soviet dictator, Joseph Stalin. (NARA)

A Fokker C.X dive-bomber of Llv 10 is pulled out of a shelter at Lappeenranta on 26 October 1939. The white circle of the national insignia was fully covered with the surrounding camouflage paint. This made the planes less conspicuous against the terrain, as the white roundels gave the aircraft away. Llv 10 was a dedicated dive-bomber outfit under the direct command of the headquarters. It was used mostly against high-value targets.

Fokker D.XXIs of Lentorykmentti 2 after the mobilization at Immola in October 1939. The national markings were tactically subdued, but disapproved of by the air force commander. The closest airplane is FR-96 belonging to LLv 26. Its two flights of Fokkers were handed over to LLv 24 on 27 November 1939.

situation was poor, and the soldiers had to wear partly civilian clothes. This outfit was called 'model Cajander' after the prime minister.

The Red Army had just over one million men on the 1,000-mile-long border against Finland. It was equipped with powerful modern artillery, strong armoury and air forces, and limitless amounts of ammunition. But this motorized army was difficult to move in a terrain with few roads. In the main front on the Karelian Ithmus, the Russians had double the number of men, north of Lake Ladoga the amount was triple, and further north it was ten times stronger. The material superiority was even greater, being ten-to-twenty-fold.

A Bristol Blenheim I bomber, serialled BL-111 of LLv 44, bellied on the first snow at Joroinen on 23 November 1939. The landing gear locks failed when the squadron CO Maj. Erik Stenbäck landed. The air force commander Maj. Gen. Jarl Lundqvist did not approve the practical, but unauthorized overpainting of the national markings and ordered them to be reinstated at the soonest opportunity, by stating, 'We fight with bright insignias.'

THE CAMPAIGN

This chapter is a day-by-day account of all notable aerial operations during the Winter War. The order of the daily presentation is: general warfare, weather, transfers and appointments (if any); LeR 1 (LLv 10, 12, 14 and 16) operations; LeR 2 (LLv 24, 26 and 28) operations; LeR 4 (LLv 42, 44 and 46) operations; LLv 36 (maritime) operations; Soviet information.

Gladiator GL-270 was assigned to 1/LLv 12 leader Capt. Auvo Maunula, who is seen here in the cockpit before take-off from Karhusjärvi, in March 1940. Maunula was a fearless and calculating reconnaissance pilot and leader, which earned him the Mannerheim Cross in the Continuation War.

December 1939

On the last day of November 1939, the Soviet Union commenced the offensive against Finland from land, sea and air. The main front was at the Karelian Isthmus, where the 7th Army attacked, over ten divisions strong, facing five Finnish divisions. Between Lake Ladoga and Porajärvi, five divisions of the 8th Army attacked, opposed by two divisions of Finns.

Further north, in the Kantalahti and Uhtua regions, the 9th Army attacked, and from Murmansk the 14th Army attacked. Here, the Finns could muster only detached battalions, three such opposing the 9th Army and another three the 14th Army. The Red Banner Baltic Fleet, Lake Ladoga Naval Detachment and the Arctic Fleet protected the flanks of the Soviet armies.

On 30 November, 200 aircraft of the Soviet air forces bombed many towns and air bases in southern Finland, while fighters cruised midway over the Karelian Isthmus. But the interceptors of LeR 2 failed to meet the invaders due to poor weather. The capital, Helsinki, was among the bombed locations, where the bombs of eight Ilyushin DB-3s of 1 AP, KBF (Aviation Regiment of the Red-Banner Baltic Fleet) caused close to 100 civilians to be killed, with another 200 wounded. This created a lot of international sympathy and goodwill for the Finns, in addition to the expulsion of the Soviet Union from the League of Nations. Ironically, modern research in the Russian archives has revealed that the downtown Helsinki bombardment took place by mistake, the actual target being the harbour and shipyard further south by the sea. LeR 4 bombers took off for long-range reconnaissance missions, but all had to be aborted due to poor weather.

SA-Kuva

An Ilyushin DB-3 escadrille above Helsinki on 30 November 1939. On this day, 1 AP, KBF bombed downtown Helsinki, killing 91 and wounding over 200 civilians. Ironically, the empty Soviet embassy also received bomb hits. They missed the actual target, which was the harbour and shipyard further south by the sea, easily distinguishable as the water was not yet frozen. (SA-kuva)

On 1 December, the army co-op squadrons of LeR 1 flew from the early morning reconnaissance missions, where the advance and spearheads of the 7th and 8th Armies could be established on both sides of Lake Ladoga. Harassment bombings were carried out whenever possible. LLv 10 was the only dive-bombing element of LeR 1 and the squadron was attached directly to General Headquarters for use against specified targets. The unit had to wait three weeks for action.

The first combat loss also occurred on this day, when Russian flak shot down at Kivennapa on the Karelian Isthmus FK-93, a reconnoitrer Fokker C.X of LLv 12, killing the pilot Sgt Urho Nissilä.

The first fighter contact was made at 1145hrs, when six Polikarpov I-16 Rata fighters of 7 IAP (Fighter Aviation Regiment) jumped a pair of Bulldogs of LLv 26. While one Bulldog got separated, the other, piloted by SSgt Toivo Uuttu in BU-64, was left alone to fight the Russians. After scoring hits on one Rata, he himself was also shot down and he crashed at Muolaanjärvi and was injured. Uuttu's victim also came down, becoming the first-ever aerial victory over Finland.

What is more, 250 unescorted bombers were in the air, again attacking many of the same targets as the day before. The Fokkers of LLv 24 took off in pairs, led by the commanding officer Capt. Gustaf Magnusson, for 59 sorties, claiming 11 bombers destroyed in Viipuri-Lappeenranta area, eight from 41 SBAP (Fast Bomber Aviation Regiment) and three from 24 SBAP.

The first bomber fell at 1205hrs under the guns of the 2nd Flight leader 1Lt Jaakko Vuorela, and the last at 1440hrs at the hands of the 5th Flight boss 1Lt Leo Ahola. Vuorela became a double scorer, while the other victors were Capt. Gustaf Magnusson, 1Lt Eino Luukkanen, 1Lt Jussi Räty, 2Lt Pekka Kokko, Sgts Lasse Heikinaro, Lauri Nissinen, Lauri Rautakorpi and Kelpo Virta, with one each. No combat reports exist from these first encounters, since the forms were not available until a couple of weeks later. However, Capt. Magnusson insisted that every pilot involved in a combat would write down his experiences on a piece of paper. His paper told the following:

Fokker FR-86 of 2/LLv 24, camouflaged under tarpaulins and white sheets at Utti on 1 December 1939. Flying this plane, the flight leader 1Lt Jaakko Vuorela opened the unit's victory score, claiming one Tupolev SB bomber of 24 SBAP shot down in the morning and another in the afternoon. The Fokkers were still on wheels as the week-old snow layer was thin. (SA-kuva)

1.12.39 at 1410–1445hrs. Based on an announcement that a Soviet bomber formation was approaching Imatra, we took off. We met the formation above Imatra. I attacked the one flying on the extreme right wing shooting first along the fuselage. When the firing did not seem to have any effect, I aimed the fire to the starboard engine, which started to smoke after a few bursts.

I had to interrupt my attack since the one on the left to my target had reduced speed being about 70 metres on my port side with the dorsal gunner firing all the time. I slowed down behind this plane and shot it into flames. The plane crashed burning into the ground.

Since the squadron did not have other than normal bullets and tracers, it was not possible to gain results with a small amount of ammunition. 1,200 rounds spent. My plane was FR-99.

This example shown by the commanding officer was much more important than anything the pilots had learnt so far. It proved that the methods used by the Finnish Air Force were sound, and nobody was willing to do less.

The squadron's first loss was tragic, when friendly anti-aircraft guns at Viipuri shot down FR-77, killing the pilot Sgt Matti Kukkonen. A further loss occurred when the squadron hack (utility aircraft), a de Havilland Moth MO-111, took a bomb hit at Immola and burned to the ground.

Both LeR 4 bomber squadrons completed their first missions. LLv 44 reconnoitred on two sorties on the traffic of the Soviet 9th Army in the Repola-Lentiera direction. LLv 46 bombed a motorized column at Säämäjärvi with three aircraft, but on the return flight, Blenheim BL-110 crashed in poor weather. On the Russian side, the fighters of 7 IAP claimed one reconnaissance aircraft shot down.

At the Arctic Sea on 2 December, the attack of the 14th Army against Petsamo (Pechenga) was repelled. On the Karelian Isthmus the forward troops withdrew towards the main defence line. The weather was very poor and most sorties had to be aborted. LLv 14 lost FK-102 in a crash caused by a snowstorm.

Poor weather would keep the interceptors of LLv 24 on the ground for almost three weeks. The fortification of the Aaland Islands began and, together with the coastal navy, LLv 36 escorted troop transfers from Turku for three days.

LLv 24 commander Maj. Gustaf Magnusson gives the Independence Day speech to his unit at Immola on 6 December 1939. Magnusson was an ace and an exceptionally capable fighter leader, which later earned him the Mannerheim Cross in the Continuation War. Behind him are Fokkers FR-105 and FR-106, both of which were soon equipped with skis.

Poor weather and snowfall continued on 3 December. Only a few reconnaissance missions could be flown. LLv 16 received an order from the IV Army Corps to – at night or dawn – bomb enemy tanks of the 8th Army, which had broken through the lines at Suvilahti. Only one tank, but a lot of infantry was seen and the aircraft faced heavy anti-aircraft artillery fire, and could not observe where the bombs hit. The lead plane received 20 bullet holes.

On 4 December, only eight reconnaissance sorties could be flown to the Karelian Isthmus. Poor weather also prevented LLv 12 from bombing tanks that were observed near Suulajärvi. The squadron's FK-101 hit trees in zero visibility and crashed.

The Soviet 8th Army advanced north of Lake Ladoga to Suojärvi on 5 December. Detachment Talvela was formed to take back the lost area. The next day, on the Karelian Isthmus, the 7th Army had pushed the Finns to the main defence line, the Mannerheim-line, and started the crossing of River Vuoksi eastwards. For three weeks, fierce battles raged at the main defence line.

LLv 16 lost Ripon RI-143 to flak on a reconnaissance mission to Äglajärvi. The crew of two was captured. Maj. Raoul Harju-Jeanty arrived to Utti and took over the command of LLv 26. Instantly, he started the preparation of the squadron for the promised new equipment – the Italian Fiat G.50 fighters. The whole of LLv 44 flew to Joroinen, which became the new base for the squadron.

North of Lake Ladoga on 7 December, the divisions of the 8th Army had advanced 50km to Uomaa at the coast and to Kollaa and Tolvajärvi further north. This was how far they would get. In the north, the 9th Army advanced to Suomussalmi and fierce battles began at Salla. LeR 4 regiment headquarters moved to Joroinen joining LLv 44.

On 8 December, LeR 1 squadrons could perform the requested reconnaissance missions on both sides of Lake Ladoga, as Soviet fighters were not observed. Fighter squadron LLv 28 was established with Maj. Niilo Jusu in command. The base was set at Säkylä in southwestern Finland and the unit began building up, until the arrival of the Morane-Saulnier M.S. 406 fighters, donated from France. The long-range reconnaissance missions by LeR 4 further north were also successful and nuisance raids against columns were pressed home due to the absence of enemy fighters.

On 9 December, LeR 1 squadrons began successful nocturnal harassment bombings against Soviet camp areas. LLv 24 transferred one flight from Immola and another from Suur-Merijoki to Lappeenranta, forming a 13-aircraft strong Detachment Vuorela. A third flight flew to Mensuvaara together with the Bulldog flight of LLv 26. One flight of LLv 46 arrived to Joroinen as reinforcement to LLv 44, in order to increase the impact on the fighting north of Lake Ladoga.

On 10 December 1939, Ripons of LLv 36 were assembled to Kallvik bay near Helsinki. Limited reconnaissance missions were flown on 11 December due to only occasionally acceptable flying weather.

The following day, Detachment Talvela stopped the advance of the 8th Army and at Tolvajärvi took a counter attack, smashing the Soviet groupings. On the western Karelian Isthmus, LLv 12 performed two reconnaissance missions, causing havoc among a motorized troop column appearing on the route. LLv 36 flew to Malmi, where the planes were fitted with wheels or skis. Due to the shortage of aircraft, the flights were united. For submarine hunting in the Baltic Sea, a Ripon pair was detached, operating in shifts, based at Turku, Pori or Maarianhamina.

On 13 December, the only action was LLv 36 conducting a submarine search on the Gulf of Bothnia. The next day the Blenheims of LLv 44 flew reconnaissance missions for Detachment Talvela, with one aircraft damaged in a forced landing and another flipped over when it landed on the snowy airfield. On 15 December, the 7th Army tried to break through the Finnish lines on the eastern Karelian Isthmus at Taipale, but was thrown back. LeR 1 squadrons flew the regular reconnaissance missions on both sides of Lake Ladoga. On 16 December, LeR 1 squadrons carried out the daily reconnaissance missions on the Karelian Isthmus and north of Lake Ladoga.

On 17 December, the 7th Army started the advance for the third time on the Karelian Isthmus at Summa-Lähde sector. In four days, the attack was repelled and the Finns destroyed, among other things, 58 tanks. Due to poor weather LLv 16 could perform only one reconnaissance mission in the far north from Rovaniemi.

On 18 December, LLv 12 flew to Konnunsuo base. A Fokker C.X pair of LLv 14 did not get to the reconnaissance area in the eastern part of the Karelian Isthmus due to enemy fighters. FK-84 became the first one to be chased by fighters, luckily at the end of the mission. The observer 2Lt Paavo Kahla reported:

> At 0925hrs 5 tanks at Luukkolanmäki heading south. No traffic on road Petäjärvi-Rautu. At 0940hrs 25–30 tanks at Mustalanmäki heading south. At Kuninkaanselkä one platoon (30 men) camping. Six trucks on Rautu-Palkeala roat at Suur-Porkku heading south-east. At 0950hrs no traffic on road Riiska-Kiviniemi. At Kellosenmäki trenches with troops shooting at the aircraft. At Rajaharju trenches with troops shooting at the aircraft. At Röykkylä one platoon camping. The pilot strafed with the forward machine-guns.

Fokker C.X, coded FK-100 of 3/LLv 12, at Suur-Merijoki in early December 1939. It was assigned to the flight leader 1Lt Aulis Bremer. He would later become a fighter pilot and ace. Under the plane's nose is a blow torch rack, hose and hood for warming the engine before starting it. Due to the C.X's simplicity, it had a good degree of serviceability under the extremely cold conditions.

At 1010hrs three enemy I-15s surprised over Noitermaa just when I was about to throw the leaflets. The trio approached from below and ahead in a wide echelon getting tighter when coming closer and firing all the time. After the pass the fighter at the extreme right made a fast Immelmann turn to continue the attack while the other two flew straight ahead. Sgt Perälä opened the throttle and avoided the contact by pulling in a shallow right turn and climb into a cloud. When we came out the enemy had gone. Altitude at the encounter was 300 metres. No hits in the aircraft. The tracers went over us, obviously too much deflection.

The Baltic Fleet air forces bombed the fortress at Saarenpää assisted by two battleships. LLv 10 received the order to dive-bomb these vessels, but arrived on the spot after the ships had already departed.

LLv 24's fighters took off for 30 sorties. Most could not engage the enemy bombers due to poor weather, but 1Lt Jorma Karhunen claimed one SB bomber of 24 SBAP shot down. LeR 4 bombed the supply centre and columns at Suojärvi with single Blenheims.

The poor weather and snowfall stopped on 19 December, resulting in an active day. The fortress of Saarenpää came under heavy aerial attacks and received about 500 bomb hits. LLv 16 sent RI-141 to reconnoitre the Äglajärvi direction, but it never came back and became missing in action. The transfer of LLv 12 to Konnunsuo base was completed. During three Finnish sorties to the western Karelian Isthmus, 25 IAP fighters shot down FK-95, killing both of the aircrew.

LLv 24 then flew 58 sorties to the front on the Karelian Isthmus and was engaged in combat on 22 occasions between 1050hrs and 1520hrs. The Soviets lost seven SBs, six thereof from 44 SBAP, and five Ilyushin DB-3s from other regiments. However, SSgt Kelpo Virta was the first in action against 25 IAP fighters and claimed two shot down. The ground troops observed both crashes and Virta was credited with two aircraft destroyed.

The squadron adjutant interviewed every pilot engaged in combat and made a summary, where the matters were told in the manner of a combat report, but a bit more freely. 1Lt Per Sovelius flew FR-92 and told this:

On 19.12.39 from 0955 to 1105hrs on air combat patrol I was leading the 3rd pair with Sgt Ikonen on my wing. We took off by the announcement. I flew over Antrea area when the radio informed 45 and I headed towards south-west. Somewhere near Kämärä I observed a 7-plane SB formation and started the chase. The SBs were flying towards south-west, but turned towards south. However, we did not gain them, but we observed a bit aside three SB planes flying roughly in the same direction.

Sgt Ikonen got well behind the plane on the starboard wing and shot it into flames from a very close range at the altitude of 2,000 metres over Kipinola. I tried to get behind the port wingman, but did not have enough speed. I observed another three SB planes heading south-west, tried after them but began to lose them. The planes were throwing leaflets.

During the chase I observed again three SB planes a little below going southwards. I picked the port wingman as my target and shot first to the rear fuselage, when the dorsal gunner quitted firing. After this I aimed the fire to the port engine, which began to smoke and finally caught fire. The plane fell to the starboard wing and dived towards the sea close to Seivästö about 10 kilometres from the coast.

I fired then at the starboard wingman, when its right engine started to pour smoke, but it stayed with the lead plane and kept going on. I did the return flight at 3,000 metres and while about 5 kilometres above the land I observed a-a [anti-aircraft] artillery explosions. On the south coast of lake Muolaanjärvi two I-16s managed to take me by surprise coming from the sun. I woke up when bullets rustled in my plane.

I pulled instantly towards them, but noticed soon that the I-16 was more manoeuvrable than the Fokker. I tried to tighten my turns, but got only once the enemy into my sight and fired a short burst. I noticed at the same time that I had ammunition left only in one gun. Once after trying to turn as tight as possible I lost the control and slipped into a spin. I continued to make all sorts of evasive actions and down at the surface I managed to shake my pursuers. I was then nearby Heinjoki.

Both I-16s attacked simultaneously and obviously in order to avoid a collision did not get straight behind me and were forced to shoot with a small deflection. Judged by the tracers the I-16s seemed to fire all the time even when my plane was clearly out of their aiming lines.

After the mission my plane had two hits. One in the tail plane and the other had gone in through the machine-gun compression bottle hatch and out from the fuselage bottom.

3/LLv 24 leader 1Lt Eino Luukkanen got a flak hit in his Fokker FR-104 on 18 December 1939, causing the engine to malfunction. In a forced landing at Kavantsaari on the snow, the heavy engine made the plane nose over. The aircraft was sent to the factory for repairs, coming back on 5 February 1940. FR-104 was one of 35 Fokker D.XXI fighters built under licence by the State Aircraft Factory.

Since the squadron adjutant took notes of every combat participant, 1Lt Urho Nieminen, on assignment from LLv 26, reported the following:

I took off at 1025hrs with four Fokkers to Viipuri direction. At Äyräpää over the railway from Leningrad I observed seven SB bombers in a formation at 2,000 metres altitude. We were 500 metres higher. We turned to the right from behind in a shallow bank.

I took the plane at extreme left as my target and shot a burst to the fuselage while 2Lt Malmivuo fired over me bursts to the left engine, setting it on fire.

I left this plane and went to chase two planes, which separated from the formation and flew south along the railway. I fired the first burst pretty far and after that several bursts to both engines. Both engines caught fire. I chased the plane up to Muolaanjärvi following its fire and descent. I saw the burning plane crash at 1050hrs between the stations of Äyräpää and Perkjärvi, just on the east side of the railway.

The planes were fast and only [the fact] that they made a full evasive circle and our altitude advantage made the catching possible. After the first bursts, the landing gear came down from both planes. The fire in the engines did not increase even if I hit with several bursts. I saw the engines of two other planes in fire. Flying time 50 minutes. My plane was FR-111.

LeR 4 reconnoitred and bombed the northeast coast of Lake Ladoga on eight sorties. For the first time, a larger number of enemy fighters were met, but the speed of the Blenheim was enough for breaking off, as on so many occasions later.

During the course of the day, 25 IAP claimed five aircraft shot down, four Fokker D.XXIs and one reconnaissance aircraft. 3 LBAP (Light Bomber Aviation Regiment) claimed a twin-engined fighter.

On 20 December 1939, LeR 1 carried out the routine reconnaissance missions to the Karelian Isthmus. Nocturnal harassment bombings of enemy camps had become a common practice. LLv 24 added two fighters and one bomber to its score on the Karelian Isthmus, while LeR 4's sorties had to be flown more often at dusk or dawn, and at a higher altitude, due to the fighter threat. Blenheim BL-106 of LLv 46 was chased by three I-16s over Salmi, when the rear gunner Sgt Viktor Mörsky managed to shoot down one attacker, the first kill to be scored by the gunners. In reply, on this same day, 7 IAP claimed four fighters shot down and 49 IAP claimed one Blenheim destroyed.

On 21 December two LeR 1 units changed bases as a precaution. In the evening, two bombing missions were flown on the Karelian Isthmus. The weather permitted flying in the morning and 300 bombers were counted over southeastern Finland. LLv 24 took off for 62 interception sorties and claimed three DB-3 bombers of 6 DBAP (Long-range Bomber Aviation Regiment) shot down on the Karelian Isthmus.

The following day, poor weather permitted only one reconnaissance mission of LLv 14 to the eastern Karelian Isthmus. However, the weather cleared on 23 December. LLv 10 dive-bombed a column at Perkjärvi with seven C.Xs, causing one truck to catch fire and breaking the column. After this the HQ kept the squadron in a reserve.

LLv 12 flew six bombing sorties to Viipuri-Leningrad railway attacking Perkjärvi station. Seven IAP fighters were directed to the target and near Johannes FK-96 was shot down, killing both of the C.X's aircrew. Bad luck hit the Soviet 44 SBAP again; between 1015hrs and 1200hrs, the Fokkers of LLv 24 downed another six SBs on the Karelian Isthmus, 1Lt Jorma Sarvanto claiming two. The squadron CO Maj. Gustaf Magnusson describes his shoot-down of one bomber in FR-99:

Sgt Kinnunen flying on the left flank observed nine SB planes above Vuoksenranta. I dived after Sgt Kinnunen, who pulled away thinking I was an I-16.

I continued after the formation and caught it at Kiviniemi. I chose as my target the rearmost bomber on the left flank. First I fired in the starboard engine, which started to smoke, thereafter I shot the port engine into fire, when the plane began to descend.

Tactically the enemy unit worked well, e.g. lowering the landing gears simultaneously for speed reduction and the next to the one under attack lowered speed in order to obtain a better firing position for its rear gunner.

At 1200hrs the aircraft hit the ground at Lempaalanjärvi.

The engagements of the day totalled 21 and, during fighter duels, two more I-16s of 7 IAP and two of 64 IAP were shot down. Sgt Pentti Tilli accounted for both of the former and 1Lt Urho Nieminen and 2Lt Heikki Ilveskorpi the latter. On the other hand, FR-111 was hit and Sgt Tauno Kaarma was injured when he crashed the D.XXI.

Lentorykmentti 2's combat summary recorded Tilli's claims thus:

Between 1050 and 1120hrs, Sergeant Tilli flew with 1Lt Luukkanen's swarm on an interception mission south-east of Viipuri. At Heinjoki the swarm destroyed one bomber out of a three-plane patrol. After this Sergeant Tilli was engaged in a combat with several fighters, firing at many. One flipped on its back, began to draw smoke and crashed between Kämärä and Heinjoki.

When returning home he saw two I-16 fighters, believing these at first to be friendly (I-16s on skis) and was engaged in a duel, where he shot one to smoke. The I-16 fell on the side and crashed down at Noskuanselkä area. Sergeant Tilli fired the others at 50–100 metres distance, but to due to a gun jamming and running out of fuel he made a successful forced landing at Kärstilänjärvi. His plane was FR-103.

Ripon RI-155 of LLv 36 was sent out to photograph the air base at Paldiski, Estonia in clear daylight. The Soviet I-153 interceptors of 5 IAP, taking off from the base, had no difficulties in shooting down the slow biplane, killing both of the aircrew.

On this very busy day, 7 IAP claimed seven fighters and one bomber shot down and 25 IAP, a further three reconnaissance aircraft and two biplanes. Over Estonia, 5 IAP, KBF (Baltic Fleet) claimed one Kotka shot down.

According to 7 IAP's war diary, from 1117 to 1226hrs, a group of 13 I-16s lead by Capt. Shinkarenko flew to cover SB operations in Viipuri area. In the region of Kaislahti at the altitude of 2,000m they saw three SBs that flew to east-north-east, and that 12 enemy aircraft (nine FRs and three BLs) flew from Nuoraa eastwards.

One enemy flight got behind the tails of the SB flight. Two SBs caught fire, while the third began to fall down disorderly. Meanwhile, Shinkarenko's squadron tried to overtake the enemy and finally caught it over Pienpero station and, at 1140hrs, entered into combat. During the course of combat the Soviet pilots claimed seven D.XXIs and one Blenheim for the loss of two I-16 (Lts Grigoryev and Zolotaryov).

On Christmas Eve, LLv 16 lost one Junkers K.43 (JU-126) in the north to the fighters, with the pilot bailing out. Continuous air combat patrols by the Russian fighters in the airspace over the Karelian Isthmus and north of Lake Ladoga made daytime reconnaissance virtually impossible, and the co-op squadrons shifted the operations to dusk, dark or dawn. Demanding and dangerous day missions were given to Fokker D.XXI fighters of LLv 24. LeR 4 carried out ten bombing sorties to Säämäjärvi area north of Lake Ladoga. In Lapland, 145 IAP claimed one Ju-21 shot down and 7 IAP, one reconnaissance aircraft on the Karelian Isthmus.

By 25 December, the Finns had stopped advances of all Soviet armies on the 1,000-mile long border, and a five-week stalemate began. The extremely cold winter, with temperatures often below 30 and on several days below 40 degrees centigrade, favoured the attacking Russians less. On Christmas Day, Fokkers of LLv 24 destroyed three Ilyushin DB-3 bombers from 6 DBAP and a Tupolev SB of 41 SBAP over the Karelian Isthmus. The 3rd Flight was strengthened to Detachment Luukkanen and transferred to Värtsilä in support of the troops on the northern coast of Lake Ladoga. There, it immediately sent down four SB bombers of 72 SBAP, with both 1Lt Jorma Karhunen and Sgt Toivo Vuorimaa claiming two. LLv 26 reported that 68 IAP then lost one I-16 fighter, as described by the Lentorykmentti 2 summary:

At 1200hrs Sergeant Porvari entered combat with 1st Lieutenant Berg over Käkisalmi with twenty I-16 fighters, when Sergeant Porvari got an opportunity to fire at one from 50 metres distance. The I-16 dodged with a manoeuvre similar to combat Immelmann, which was cut as the plane flipped into a dive. After a couple of spins the plane flew straight again. Sergeant Porvari could not follow it longer due to the attack of other I-16s. His plane was BU-68.

Detachment Luukkanen of LLv 24 at Värtsilä on Christmas Day of 1939. From left: mech, armourer, mech P. Hannula, mech J. Paajanen, Sgt I. Juutilainen, mech Karhu, SSgt P. Tilli, mech P. Heino, 1Lt T. Huhanantti, mech Eve, 1Lt E. Luukkanen, mech J. Raunio, 1Lt J. Karhunen, mech K. Pyötsiä and mech E. Horppu. The unit's transfers to operate north of Lake Ladoga came as a surprise to the freely-operating Red air forces, which lost four SB bombers in the first encounter.

68 IAP claimed two fighters and one reconnaissance aircraft. 26 IAP claimed in three encounters two Gamecocks and two Bulldogs, during the two missions it flew that day. During the first one, 24 I-16s escorted 32 SBs of 24 SBAP to Käkisalmi. At the approach to Kakisalmi, 15 I-16s, led by deputy commander of 26 IAP Capt. Dervyanov, were attacked by two Gamecocks. His report reads:

At 1300–1310hrs when the group was turning towards the target in the region of Keksgolm (Käkisalmi), I saw two biplane aircraft of Gloster Gamecock type behind me, diving towards me from the altitude of 300m. I turned to right climbing up and attacked the closest. I fired one burst and the enemy fighters passed me on both sides and went into a turn. When I completed the turn one enemy passed in front of me banking 70–75 degrees. I gave a long burst and enemy turned over the wing and disorderly flew towards the ground. I overtook him at the altitude of 700m and fired one more burst, after which it began to fall down and disappeared.

The second Gamecock was attacked by fighters of the first and the second flights and broke off to the clouds. At 1310–1320hrs, another group of nine I-16s led by the commander of 54 IAB, Col. A. S. Blagoveshchenskiy, also met one Gamecock at the approach to Käkisalmi and supposedly shot it down.

During the second mission, 18 I-16s attacked Käkisalmi airfield in two groups. Between 1525 and 1535hrs, the first nine I-16s lead by Blagoveshchenskiy met two lone Gamecocks, which evaded combat and escaped to the clouds. Since Käkisalmi airfield was covered with clouds, the fighters did not attack and returned home. Between 1530 and 1540hrs, the second group of eight I-16s led by StLt Gorokhov met a lone Gamecock in the Suvantojärvi region, which evaded combat and disappeared. Then the I-16s met another Gamecock and StLt Storozhakov shot it down.

The next day, it turned out that the downed Gamecock was actually an I-15bis of 59 IAB, which had made a forced landing in friendly territory. During the same flight the squadron met several R-5s, one of which was fired at by mistake. To complete this unfortunate mission, the squadron was fired on by heavy anti-aircraft machine-gun fire during its return flight, 6–10km north of Suvantojärvi. In return, the squadron strafed the machine-gun positions. In this exchange of fire, I-16 No. 231 was hit and went down in Rahkajärvi. Pilot MlLt Masurenko was killed. Due to adverse weather this group also failed to attack Käkisalmi airfield.

On 26 December, the Finnish 9th Division destroyed completely one division of the Soviet 9th Army at Suomussalmi, while LLv 24 fighters flew almost 50 sorties, but the Red Army air force bombers evaded contact. The next day, LeR 1 squadrons continued nocturnal reconnaissance and harassment bombardments on the Karelian Isthmus, and the Soviets lost three SB bombers of 2 SBAP. WO Viktor Pyötsiä shot down two Polikarpov I-15bis fighters north of Lake Ladoga, writing in the combat report:

3/LLv 24 leader 1Lt Eino Luukkanen sitting in his Fokker during December 1940. He commanded this flight throughout the Winter War, claiming two whole and one shared air victory. Later in the Continuation War, he became an ace flying Brewster 239s and Messerschmitt Bf 109Gs, with the third biggest score of 54 enemy aircraft. Luukkanen was also a Mannerheim Cross recipient.

At 1430hrs. I flew westwards with Sgt Mannila east of Suojärvi, when a solitary plane arrived from south-east. We gained altitude and when the plane started to follow Sgt Mannila, I dived from the side and fired a burst. It caught fire and went down burning, to the west coast of Salonjärvi. The pilot bailed out in a 40-degree dive and opened his parachute.

At the same time another plane arrived behind me starting shooting. I pulled up, the plane followed shooting but missed. I dived towards it not being able to shoot. Sgt Mannila dived and shot. In the pull out he went into a spin, likewise the Russki. After levelling the Russki climbed again towards. I dived like earlier and fired a burst. Soon a flame began to blink behind the engine, the plane started to descend. Sgt Mannila dived and fired long bursts at it during the glide. The plane landed at the south end of Salonjärvi in the middle of open ice.

The plane is inferior in climb to Fokker. More manoeuvrable than I-16. Considerably fast but slower than I-16. Had no problems attacking from below. Four machine-guns in the fuselage, shot during pull up. Plane in dark colour, Soviet stars, no bands on wings. My plane was FR-110.

This turned out to be the busiest day for LeR 4 so far. LLv 44 flew seven sorties to the Tulemajärvi-Käsnäselkä area, during which the front line was photographed and bombed. LLv 46 extended one recce sortie to Kiantajärvi and Capt. Kalle Kepsu bombed a motorized column twice with three aircraft in Ilomantsi area, scoring good hits among the trucks. Kepsu's bombing report said:

At 1445–1450hrs bombed with three aircraft (BL-112, 106 and 108) Valasmo village east of Porajärvi, target being 30–40 trucks parked on the road between the houses. Bombing height 800 metres. Full hits in the village and column. Two houses blew up and the whole area was covered with smoke. Plenty of troops at Porajärvi and an anti-aircraft machine-gun on the ice. In the woods east of Kinnasjärvi lake lots of troops camping at the road plus an unspecified amount of trucks. The aircraft were shot at from several locations. Three large fires at Porajärvi, caused by bombings.

Two Ripons of LLv 36 bombed the lighthouse of Ruuskeri, west of Suursaari (Gogland), with hits being recorded in the nearby buildings.

On 28 December, as Immola air base was frequently a target for the Soviet bombers, the headquarters and two flights of LLv 24 moved to Joutseno. The next day, poor weather permitted only a few routine missions by each regiment. Poor weather continued on 30 December, with only LLv 12 able to fly two reconnaissance missions on the western Karelian Isthmus.

On the last day of the year Sgt Ilmari Juutilainen, member of LLv 24's Detachment Luukkanen and the future top scorer with 94 kills, blasted behind 1Lt Karhunen's tail a lone I-16 on the northern shore of Lake Ladoga. Juutilainen's combat report said:

> At 1030hrs. We were flying in a search formation when I observed above left between the clouds two enemy I-16s. I did not see other planes, but there were three more in the clouds. I got behind the lead plane to 150m distance, when it noticed me. I shot at it in a bank and then we circled around each other. When it started to get behind my tail I pulled up and banked into the cloud. There I turned swiftly to the opposite direction and came out of the cloud 150m behind the enemy. The enemy observed me when I was 100m behind and when I opened fire towards it. I followed down to 50m shooting long bursts. The I-16 poured heavy smoke and went under me in a gliding turn. After this I could not see it anywhere, not above or below the clouds.
>
> The wreck was found at Syskyjärvi. The enemy plane was dark and both wings and fuselage had red stars. The landing gear was in. The machine guns, two in the fuselage and one in each wing, fired straight ahead, with tracers in every gun. I observed this when it was shooting at 1Lt Karhunen from 500–600m distance, being myself 200m behind the enemy. My plane was FR-106.

LLv 24 scored steadily and the first month of operations showed 54 enemy aircraft sent down for the cost of only one Fokker lost and another damaged. The small number of available fighters permitted the interception over the Karelian Isthmus, but did not allow the interception of almost daily air raids of southern Finland, where numerous bombers attacked many locations.

A five-strong Bulldog detachment of LLv 26 led by Capt. Erkki Heinilä flew to Littoinen near Turku, to defend the important ports of Turku, Rauma and Pori in southwestern Finland.

January 1940

The first month of the war had gone better than anticipated for the Finns. On the Karelian Isthmus the advance was stopped at the main defensive line. Between Lake Ladoga and the Arctic Sea, the Soviet troops were forced to a standstill despite Finnish difficulties at the beginning. North of Lake Ladoga the Finns had started to gain territory back. At Suomussalmi the battles ended in an effective victory which lasted for the rest of the war. At Salla, all advances were stopped permanently.

The Soviet bombardments on Finnish cities and towns had proven to be less effective that assumed. The activities of the Red Banner Baltic Fleet on the left flank had shown to be ineffective and of little threat. The Soviet supreme command had ordered a halt to all offensives and took action to concentrate troops on the Karelian Isthmus, forming the northwestern front, consisting of the 7th and 13th Armies.

On 1 January the main part of LLv 24 flew to Utti. It was discovered that the Soviet bombers orienteered by the aid of the Finnish railway network on their way to attack targets in the inner parts of the country. North of Lake Ladoga, the Fokkers of LLv 24 scored three bombers shot down. One victor was 1Lt Jorma Karhunen reporting this:

At 1255hrs. We were with Sgt Vuorimaa on an interception mission when I observed five SB bombers heading to Leppäsyrjä. They turned to the south-east and we chased them in the Muhujärvi direction, where the firefight commenced. In the shooting the outer left-wing plane caught fire and I then fired at the lead plane of a trio, which soon started to pour heavy black smoke from the starboard engine and began to lose altitude.

Sgt Vuorimaa fired all the time at the outer right-wing plane, which departed from the formation. The enemy tried to escape by climbing through a layer of clouds and flew then just under the ceiling of the clouds. The burning plane refused to leave the formation and used the nose guns to shoot at me. My plane was FR-112.

On 2 January, the Finnish 9th Division destroyed the second division of the Soviet 9th Army in the area of Suomussalmi. Among other things, 100 pieces of field artillery and 43 tanks were captured.

On 3 January poor weather permitted only a few routine missions by LeR 1 reconnaissance planes and LeR 2 interceptors. The next day, only a few routine missions were flown to both sides of Lake Ladoga, and 10 ABr, KBF claimed one Bulldog over southwestern Finland. On 5 January, LLv 24 fighters carried out 35 interception sorties, claiming four bombers shot down over the Karelian Isthmus. On assignment from LLv 26, 2Lt Olli Puhakka gave the following report of his claim:

At 1130hrs. I led two pairs. Sgt Fräntilä on my wing observed first six enemy planes a little lower and aside north of Karhusuo. He banked in front of me after them. I started to follow the formation with MSgt Rimminen, the others remaining behind. It was almost impossible to catch the enemy planes, even when I occasionally flew 2,000m higher than they. Over Mikkeli the distance had shorted enough so that I could make a dive. During it I observed that three more planes had joined the formation. I could have been able to attack these, but the engine quitted after the dive.

After efforts the engine began to run normally, but the enemy planes had turned back and I did not have the time to make a short cut. During the return flight I was able to get by diving into a firing position 150m behind one bomber. I shot at the fuselage and port engine, which instantly caught fire. At the same time the plane went into a bank, which soon turned to an almost vertical dive. The port engine burned with a long flame.

I stopped following this and began to chase eight other planes, I caught the one on the outer right wing, spending most of my ammunition in it. It lost speed so that I was twice close ramming it, because of the poor visibility caused by the enemy's leaking oil covering my plane's forward fuselage. Hatches and other stuff also flew off the plane.

When out of ammunition and with 40 litres of fuel left I turned towards the base. This occurred south-east of Nuijamaanjärvi. When I left the plane both its engines were smoking and it had stayed below and behind its formation. I did not pay attention to the exact locations since there was no possibility of getting disoriented. During the chase the lead patrol tried to evade the fighters by starting a turn. When the fighters began the shortcut the bombers returned quickly to the earlier course. My plane was FR-117.

North of Lake Ladoga, 49 IAP claimed two Blenheims on two occasions. At 1032–1120hrs, six I-16s of 49 IAP escorted three groups of SB bombers to the area of Suistamo. At 1100hrs near Läskelä, when the first group of six SB was flying to north-west, a lone Blenheim approached this group from the north. The Blenheim flew below the group and its gunner opened fire towards the SB. Two I-16s (Lt Bobrov and MlLt Goryunov) attacked the Blenheim, flying in the Suistamo direction, along of the eastern bank of Jänisjärvi. The fighters pursued and attacked the Blenheim all the way to Juuttulampi where, emitting black smoke, it began to descend steeply and disappeared in the forest.

Another encounter took place at 1150hrs, 7km northwest of Salmi, when three I-16s attacked a lone Blenheim, which used the dense haze to disengage in the Valamo direction.

In the morning of 6 January, 17 Ilyushin DB-3Ms of 6 DBAP took off in two detachments from Estonia to bomb Kuopio in eastern Finland. The first nine planes bombed as planned, but the second formation of eight bombers drifted too far west in the crosswind and crossed the Gulf of Finland south of Utti, where 4/LLv 24 was then based. 1Lt Per Sovelius was in the air, caught the bombers at 1010hrs and sent one down on the left flank.

The remaining seven continued to Kuopio, released the bombs (which did not cause any serious damage), and returned the same route along the railway. 1Lt Jorma Sarvanto had meanwhile taken off and met the bombers. His extended combat report describes those famous four minutes as follows:

The 4th Flight of LLv 24, consisting of six Fokker D.XXIs, was temporarily posted to Utti from 1 January 1940 onwards. The task was to intercept bomber streams flying to inner parts of the country via Kouvola. The flight was led by the squadron commander Maj. Magnusson aside his main post. The weather was usually cloudy and the search for the bombers had failed during the past couple of days.

At Epiphany, 6 January 1940, the weather favoured the enemy's bombing missions. In the morning there was a layer of clouds from 300 to 400 metres altitude, with gaps here and there. Above it was a peculiar dim layer, which extended to 4,000–5,000 metres altitude. The horizontal visibility sideways was very limited.

I was leading the second patrol, to which in addition to myself belonged 2Lt Olli Mustonen. My patrol carried out a search of bombers in the morning but found no enemies. On the other hand 1Lt Per Sovelius, who was coming from Lappeenranta to Utti, heard via radio the messages sent to us, and based on them found the bombers at 3,000 metres on the way to the north. He attacked from behind and fired at the two extreme left machines, of which one caught fire and dived to the ground.

After 1040hrs no announcements of enemy aircraft were received. We had a breakfast in all peace at the back hangar at Utti, with the machines covered in front of the hangar. My patrol was the first to take off if an alert came. Next was the patrol of 1Lt Sovelius and last that of Maj. Magnusson. All had the same readiness anyway.

While eating it struck me that possibly those bombers attacked by 1Lt Sovelius were returning along the same route and therefore we could increase our readiness. I informed the others and went out, leaving my breakfast half way. I ordered the mechanics to start the engine. I also put my parachute on.

Then an announcement came by phone that from north at Mikkeli level seven bombers were coming southwards, following the railway. I shouted: 'Second patrol to the planes'. I ran to my plane and jumped in the cockpit, and as a first action switched the radio on.

The radio gave announcements and they were very accurate, square by square on the map, allowing me to follow the flight of the enemy bombers. I observed that they were coming straight towards our base at Utti. I also paid attention to the time delay of the communication, which from experience I knew would cause the planes to be already in the next square when the message came.

I heard from the radio 'sit', which meant an order for take-off. The mechanic of my wingman ran to me and informed that the engine of Mustonen's plane did not start. I pushed the throttle to fully open and took off from the platform straight across the airfield towards north. My plane was at the best climbing angle, moving me up and forward at 170km/h.

1Lt Jorma Sarvanto of 4/LLv 24 in the cockpit of his FR-97 'white 2' at Utti, right after the very successful mission on 6 January 1940, when he downed six DB-3 bombers of 6 DBAP in just four minutes. All wrecks were found at a distance of 28km between Utti and Tavastila. FR-97 had 23 bullet holes, none very serious, but was still flown to the repair shop.

The weather had improved since the morning. The lower cloud layers were gone and the sun was shining. The dim layer was still there. During the whole climb I listened to the radio and the messages were very clear. No other announcements than those of the approaching seven bombers came in. I took a few glimpses behind me and found to be alone.

When I looked up and forward I observed the light bellies of the bomber line. The colour of the machines matched well the blue of the sky behind, realizing that from a greater distance I would not have observed them. I was a few hundred metres lower than the bombers and I turned to the south, when they were left behind me. I kept the best climbing angle and watched at the bombers when they went over me with a considerable speed. For a moment I was in the firing sector of the nose gunners just 200–300 metres away, but I did not observe anyone open fire. I climbed further but now reduced the angle and ended at about 600 metres behind the bombers at the same altitude.

The throttle was still fully open, as it had been from the beginning of the flight. The altimeter showed 2,000 metres and the clock 1200hrs. I closed the mixture lever a little in order to get the maximum power from the engine. I deduced from the noise of the engine that it was running at full power. I switched off the radio so that the messages would not

Sarvanto: Ace in a day, 6 January 1940

On this day, 6 DBAP took off from Krechevichy with 17 Ilyushin DB-3 bombers in two detachments to bomb the ammunition factory and traffic junction at Kuopio. The first detachment of nine planes led by Maj. Balashov carried out the attack without interference and returned to its base. The second detachment of eight DB-3s, headed by Maj. Maistrenko, drifted in the side wind too far to the east and crossed the coast at Kotka. Six Fokkers of 4/LLv 24 were stationed at Utti near Kouvola, based on the information that the Soviet bombers had been orienteering to the targets in the inner parts of Finland by the railway network. In this case, it was the rail from Kouvola via Mikkeli to Kuopio. When Maistrenko's formation approached Kouvola, 1Lt Per Sovelius was flying from Lappeenranta to Utti and engaged the bombers, shooting one down. The remaining seven continued to Kuopio, bombed without any significant effects and then returned the same way.

Now, 1Lt Jorma Sarvanto had taken off, alone since his wingman's aircraft refused to start. He met the bombers above Utti at 2,000 metres altitude and began shooting at 1203hrs. Four minutes later, he had destroyed six bombers. The last one escaped, but not for long since 1Lt Sovelius, after refuelling and rearming, had scrambled and caught the bomber over the Gulf of Finland, sending it down between Suursaari and Lavansaari. The wrecks of all six victims of Sarvato were found, and they fell on a distance of 28km. As a result of the action, 22 Soviet airmen were killed, including Maistrenko, and two became prisoners of war.

disturb me as this seemed now unnecessary. I also took occasional glimpses behind me to avoid possible surprises. I checked all four machine-guns, compressed air bottle settings and opened the protective cap of the Goerz optical sight.

In level flight I had gradually caught up the seven bombers in front of me. With the sight I estimated the distance to be 500 metres. The bombers flew almost in a straight line and only one plane length apart. At left was a slightly backwards staggered echelon and from there to the right all others in a line. There was hardly any stagger vertically.

I approached the bombers so that I was simultaneously in a dead angle of the tails of the two bombers at the extreme left. The third from left appeared to be the most dangerous. I was wishing that the dorsal gunners were at ease after a long bombing mission, but from 300 metres my plane began to rattle unpleasantly and tracers flew all around. I had flown straight ahead up to now but now I swung my plane in order to hinder the aim of the gunners. I was still approaching with a good speed and the extreme left bomber was in the sight.

The distance was now 200 metres, when I fired the first short burst, which seemed to hit. Then I turned my plane and fired at the third from the left. A short burst silenced the gunner. I gave a similar burst to the second plane from the left. I was now about 100 metres behind them and the extreme left plane was lightly smoking. I shot a couple of short bursts into the smoking engine, which caught fire. Then I shot the third from left into flames from close range.

The earlier defence tactics of the bombers used to be that when a fighter was firing at the left wing, one or more on the right wing dropped back, moving behind the fighter and giving the nose gunner an opportunity for firing. To avoid this I swung my plane to the right wing of the formation and continued shooting short bursts, first at the most dangerous dorsal gunners and then into the starboard engines.

Fighter pilots of LLv 24 on the New Year's Day of 1940. On this day, the 1st and 4th Flights moved from Joutseno to Utti. Standing from left WO Y. Turkka, Sgt L. Heikinaro, 1Lt J. Sarvanto and Danish volunteer 1Lt E. Frijs. Sitting from left Sgt R. Heiramo, Sgt E. Kinnunen and Sgt T. Kaarma. Behind is Fokker FR-81, which was shot down over Ruokolahti on 2 February 1940, killing Danish volunteer 1Lt Frits Rasmussen.

The extreme right plane pulled up to the right, departing the formation and smoking heavily. I left it alone and continued my work as before. When I looked at right I observed that the departed plane was already in flames and was going into a spin to the death.

During the duel I only used short bursts and never fired unless I was certain of hitting. It was not too difficult as the firing distance was mostly under 50 metres, on occasion just the length of the bomber. As far as I can remember only part of one burst went under the wing when the pilot pulled tightly up.

The reddish January sun shone towards me all the time through the dim layer, unless covered by the smoke of hit planes. At the beginning the enemy bombers were flying to south-east, but then tried to take advantage of the sun turning straight to the south against the sun.

Shooting down the sixth bomber took the longest time. I did a good job since in the dorsal turret of the seventh plane was an already a dead gunner. I shot at very close range and in bursts that were a bit longer. Now only the synchronized fuselage guns worked since the wing guns with higher rate of fire had run out of ammunition. The sixth bomber finally caught fire and I moved right behind the last one. I aimed from above and behind to the starboard engine and pulled the trigger.

The guns were silent. I did the cocking procedures but with no results. I was out of ammunition and there was nothing else to do than to turn back home.

All the DB-3s crashed between Utti and Tavastila, a distance of 28km. Sarvanto was credited with six victories in four minutes and became the first ace of the Finnish Air Force. His Fokker FR-97 had taken 23 hits, none very serious, but was still flown to the repair shop. This attracted the interest of foreign media, as nothing like this had happened before in Europe.

The last DB-3 was chased to the Gulf of Finland by 1Lt Sovelius, who in the meantime had refuelled and rearmed. He shot it down at 1230hrs, between Lavansaari and Suursaari.

In other events that day, LeR 4 flew five sorties to bomb supply columns in the rear of the 8th Army. The defending fighters shot down Blenheim BL-112 of LLv 46. The aircrew bailed out and returned by foot through the lines. Again, 49 IAP claimed one Blenheim shot down, while 6 DBAP claimed eight Fokker D.XXIs destroyed and 18 SBAP one more.

The weather was very cold on 7 January, with temperatures below minus 40 degrees centigrade. Two flights of LLv 24 returned to Joutseno. One Ripon of LLv 36, carrying out a scouting sortie over the Gulf of Finland, observed a submarine on the surface. Both opened fire and when the Russian vessel submerged, the Finns dropped one depth charge which detonated 40m from the boat. From Russian sources, it was learnt that the boat was N-77, which escaped without any damage.

On 8 January, LLv 36 carried out only three reconnaissance sorties to the Sea of Aaland in the west, and, the next day, LeR 1 took off for one sortie to the Karelian Isthmus and three sorties north of Lake Ladoga. LLv 36 flew five sorties north of Aaland.

On 10 January, the main part of LLv 10 was transferred to Mensuvaara and the sorties were directed north of Lake Ladoga. LLv 22 was established at Hollola with Capt. Erkki Heinilä in command. On this same day, 44 Brewster Model 239s were ordered from the United States, but these would arrive too late to see action. Northern Finland also got its own air force, when Swedish volunteer unit Flygflottilj 19 arrived at Kemi, commanded by Maj. Hugo Beckhammar. This unit consisted of 12 Gladiator fighters and four Hart light bombers. Forward bases were established at Rovaniemi, Kemijärvi, Oulu, Vaala and Posio.

1Lt Jorma Sarvanto holds the rudder fabric of one of the six DB-3 bombers he shot down on 6 January 1940. This was the first ace-on-a-mission case in Europe and it attracted considerable international interest. Both domestic and foreign reporters attended the press occasion, which was held at Utti officers' club two days later. (SA-kuva

Unsuitable flying weather continued on 11 January. Only LLv 14 took off for one sortie to the eastern Karelian Isthmus. In the west, LLv 36 flew three maritime reconnaissance sorties. 13 IAP, KBF claimed one Fokker shot down in the Kotka area.

However, the weather cleared on 12 January, and about 400 bombers were counted over southern Finland. In Lapland, F 19 flew its first mission, when four Harts escorted by four Gladiators bombed first a column at Salmijärvi and then Märkäjärvi air base, where three I-15bis fighters were destroyed. Several Soviet fighters climbed to intercept and the Gladiators shot one down. After the bombardment, two Harts collided in the air and three fighters shot down a third. In Lapland, 145 IAP claimed one aircraft shot down.

On 13 January, two Ripons bombed a Russian icebreaker east of Suursaari, without scoring any hits.

At Tampere, inland in southern Finland, the State Aircraft Factory was located. It had been a target of several Soviet air attacks, but with no results. From here, the Test Flight began interception missions using repaired aircraft, which were flown by either the test pilots or by fighter pilots collecting planes from the factory. The Test Flight had also received two Fiat G.50 fighters from Italy. Capt. Olavi Ehrnrooth scored one SB bomber on this day, the unit's first claim.

On 14 January, an estimated 300 Soviet bombers attacked over southern and inner Finland. The bombers had free access from bases in Estonia and south of Leningrad, flying over the Gulf of Finland. Occasional snowstorms prevented most flying at the fronts, while 53 DBAP claimed one fighter shot down.

Along the coast road, north of Lake Ladoga, the Soviet 8th Army was threatened with being completely besieged. It did not retreat, however, and was cut into small *motti* encirclements (a Finnish tactic of circling the enemy into pockets). On 15 January, LLv 10 bombed the encirclement at Lemetti with single aircraft, while defending fighters shot down a Fokker C.X (FK-87), killing both of the aircrew. 49 IAP claimed one Fokker C.X, shot down north of Lake Ladoga. On 16 January, LeR 1 and LeR 4 bombed columns and encirclements on the coast road north of Lake Ladoga, while SSgt Pentti Tilli of LLv 24 claimed one SB bomber in the area.

With temperatures below minus 40 degrees centigrade, 17 January was a very cold day. Maj. Otto Holm took command of LLv 12. Ten Fokkers of LLv 24 scrambled and, at 1355hrs, caught 25 SBs of 54 SBAP returning in three formations via the Karelian

Isthmus. Within 25 minutes, ten bombers had met their end and several more were damaged. SSgt Kelpo Virta claimed his fifth air victory, becoming an ace. 2Lt Olli Puhakka continued to score this way:

I was alone coming from Muolaanjärvi and flying towards Antrea. From the Lappeenranta direction came six SB bombers, chased by two or three Fokkers at 4,000m altitude. I dived with a semi-roll after the lead plane of the rearmost trio. The firing had no visual effect. After pulling up I saw that its starboard engine had started smoking. Simultaneously I saw that the other Fokkers had shot one bomber into flames and during the dive one man had bailed out.

I attacked the foremost patrol, because the other Fokkers were behind the formation. I first fired at the right-wing plane, the starboard engine caught instantly fire and the plane began to descend, when I left it. Later I saw that the fire had extinguished and the plane was behind and 1,000m below the others.

Then I shot at the lead plane when the port engine started to smoke. Then I fired the rest of my bullets into the left-wing plane. At this point its port engine was burning and the starboard one smoking and the landing gear came down.

Armour-piercing bullets remained unused since after a couple of shots a bullet was stuck in the barrel. One wing gun sent only 200 rounds because the belt links had blocked the exit hole. My plane was FR-117.

This was the last occasion when the Finnish fighters met unescorted bombers and claimed in numbers. Thereafter the recently introduced fighter escort made scoring much more difficult.

The most significant Swedish contribution was sending a flying unit, Flygflottilj 19, which arrived to Veitsiluoto on 12 January 1940. F 19 was composed of 12 Gladiators and four Harts. It took over the air defence of Lapland, which previously had none. At left is the unit commander, Maj. Hugo Beckhammar and chief of staff, Capt. Björn Bjuggren.

Pilots of 1/LLv 24 and 4/LLv 24 at Joutseno in January 1940. From left 2Lt O. Mustonen, 2Lt I. Törrönen, WO Y. Turkka, 1Lt P. Sovelius, Sgt E. Kinnunen, MSgt S. Ikonen, 2Lt T. Vuorimaa, Sgt M. Alho and Sgt L. Heikinaro. All these fighter pilots made claims during the Winter War, with Sovelius, Turkka and Vuorimaa becoming aces with five kills or more.

Pilots of LLv 24 at Joutseno in front of Fokker FR-110 in January 1940. From left Sgt M. Alho, 2Lt T. Harmaja, 1Lt J. Räty, 1Lt V. Karu, squadron commander Maj. G. Magnusson, WO V. Pyötsiä, MSgt S. Ikonen, 1Lt P. Sovelius, 2Lt I. Törrönen and a war correspondent. Of these men, Karu and Magnusson later became Mannerheim Cross holders in the Continuation War.

In the north, the Gladiators of F19 shot down two fighters from 145 IAP during a reconnaissance mission to Salla, while 54 SBAP claimed 11 fighters shot down in the Lappeenranta area. In reality, the figures were quite the opposite, as on so many other occasions.

On 18 January, over 450 bombers were observed over southern Finland, with the ports on the southwest being especially heavily attacked. The fighters of LLv 24 took off for 47 sorties, but failed to meet the enemy. Other units carried out the regular missions.

The next day, LLv 10 performed three dive-bombing missions north of Lake Ladoga. In the morning four planes attacked a 20-truck column in the opens at Uusikylä. Bomb hits were observed in the middle of the column and at the end of it. A 40-truck column was observed at Uuksu. After refuelling and rearming, four planes struck this column two hours later, and all four scored hits in the column.

On the third occasion, the squadron dive-bombed motorized troops packed into the Pitkäranta industrial area. Seven Fokker C.Xs led by 1Lt Aimo Pietarinen caused great confusion among the Russians, destroying several trucks and buildings. The bombing report stated:

Aircraft and crews: FK-88 1Lt Pietarinen and Sgt Kirjavainen, FK-89 WO Hämelä and 1Lt Bärlund, FK-108 1Lt Nurminen and Cpl Laine, FK-111 2Lt Nenonen and 2Lt Roschier, FK-81 WO Heilä and Sgt Peltonen, FK-85 Sgt Rekola and 2Lt Rahko and FK-86 SSgt Louko and 1Lt Vaittinen. The dive-bombing was done from 600 metres at 1233hrs. Bombs 2x 100kg, 12x 50kg and 48x 25kg, release at 0.2 second intervals.

Results: Crew 1: Large drying building, full hit. Crew 2: Trucks in front of the drying building, bombs in the middle of the crowd. Crew 3: Large shack and trucks at the junction, all destroyed. Crew 4: Long building north of the cellulose factory, hit by two 50kg bombs. 25kg bombs hit the trucks parked next to the building. Crew 5: Alley between the buildings full of trucks, all bombs on the trucks. Crew 6: Five houses east of the southern log yard, full hits in three, plenty of troops running away. Crew 7: Three houses west of the same yard, all hit, plenty of troops running around.

At dusk, on four occasions and with nine sorties LLv 12 bombed a base on the ice of Lake Kirkkojärvi, which held 12 I-16 fighters. The bombs were seen to have hit eight of them. LLv 24 gained a new ace, 1Lt Urho Nieminen, who achieved the status by shooting down an SB bomber on the Karelian Isthmus. Future 46-victory ace and Mannerheim Cross winner, 2Lt Olli Puhakka was building up his score in this manner:

At 1350hrs we took off from the base with six fighters heading to Sakkola, led by 1Lt Nieminen. At Sakkola came towards us below us from east to west three SB bombers on skis, flying in a tight echelon. 1Lt Nieminen and SSgt Virta attacked first. I took a steep dive and attacked the lead plane opening fire. When I passed them underneath I noticed that I also passed the whole group. I then pulled up to left and waited a moment, seeing that all planes were under fire and one already smoking.

Two on the left flank began to turn over Suvanto. The right-wing plane was delayed a bit when I dived and got right behind it for an attack. I fired a few short bursts when the port engine and lower fuselage gave a big flame. Also the starboard engine started to smoke, showing small flames. I pulled away because I thought that the plane would break up in front of me, it being in flames, heavily smoking and pouring oil over me. However, I saw that it continued to fly on fire in a shallow glide going south of Kiviniemi.

The other two SBs were considerably ahead of it and above left, both smoking. Behind them was one Fokker (SSgt Virta). I saw other Fokkers north of Suvanto, flew there and began the return flight. I landed at 1450hrs. I had used 400 rounds. All guns were working. My plane was FR-117.

Another with success was SSgt Oiva Tuominen, who claimed one bomber:

At 1430hrs. I attacked a three-plane enemy formation. I first shot at the dorsal turret of the rearmost left-wing plane. SSgt Virta had just before shot the port engine into flames. I pulled up when I observed two enemy planes of another formation climbing into a cloud. Before entering the cloud I saw at right SSgt Virta shoot both engines into flames in a shallow dive.

When I came above the clouds the two SBs also came out of the clouds a little left to me and banked to the right. I fired from left a burst at the left plane, which instantly pulled into a climbing bank and fell into a dive.

The other went into the clouds and me after, but I could not catch it. I saw the plane that I had shot crash on the shore of Lake Ladoga. My plane was FR-86.

The heavy scoring caused the airspace over southeastern Finland to became almost free of bombers for the next two weeks.

Also on this day, LLv 44 lost Blenheim BL-121 with its three-man aircrew on a reconnaissance and harassment bombing mission to the north of Lake Ladoga. A Blenheim of LLv 46 observed at Lake Karkunlampi an air base on the ice, with 60–70 aircraft parked in two rows. Bombs were dropped on the rows. On the Russian side, for once records agree, with 49 IAP claimed one Blenheim shot down.

On 20 January LLv 10 sent four dive-bombers to attack truck columns on Pitkäranta-Salmi road. The patrolling I-16 fighters prevented the unit bombing, with all planes operating individually. All were chased by two fighters, disturbing the actual bombing, but several bombs were seen hitting the column or very close. The low-laying clouds offered the protection and escape.

Pilots of 4/LLv 24 at Joutseno in January 1940, in front of the commander, Maj. Gustaf Magnusson's personal fighter FR-99 'black 1'. From left: Sgt Martti Alho, Danish volunteer 1Lt Frits Rasmussen, 2Lt Tapani Harmaja and 1Lt Per Sovelius. Early next month, both Rasmussen and Harmaja would lose their lives in fighter duels.

Detachment Luukkanen of LLv 24 engaged north of Lake Ladoga bombers of three regiments, both arriving and departing and succeeded in destroying five of them. WO Viktor Pyötsiä scored two and SSgt Pentti Tilli one, both becoming aces. Then, the luck turned and two I-16s appeared on the scene to chase the Finnish Fokkers and Tilli was shot down to death. Pyötsiä's report read:

At 1420hrs. Eight-plane SB squadron over Korpiselkä at 4,000 metres. I attacked two bombers on the left flank, shooting at the first without visible results. I then attacked the outmost plane on the right flank. After firing the port engine started to smoke. I then moved back to the left flank and shot without any results. Again behind the smoking plane, a burst to the starboard engine, which caught fire. The plane banked to the left, began a dive and disintegrated in the air. One man bailed out.

I followed the other planes shooting in turns at the four rearmost planes. I managed to get puffs of smoke but not continuous smoking. At the end of Tolvajärvi I ran out of ammunition, so I turned home.

At Tolvajärvi the wrecks of two SBs were found, shot down by fighters. My plane had nine bullet hits, among others in the left-wing gun magazine, where one incendiary round burned, causing jamming to the gun. The propeller was hit with an armour-piercing bullet, which was stuck in it. My plane was FR-110.

1Lt Tatu Huhanantti took off at Tampere in one Fokker D.XXI, which had been under repair at the State Aircraft Factory. On the way back to the base, he met three SB bombers belonging to 35 SBAP and quickly shot down two before the escort of five I-153s could interfere. The wrecks were easily found as the planes came down next to the railway line, 60km north of Helsinki.

In the morning, Maj. Erik Stenbäck of LLv 44 attacked the Karkunlampi base with four Blenheims and scored several hits among the parked aircraft, just in time, before enemy fighters appeared on the scene. His reconnaissance and bombing report stated shortly:

At 0920hrs on Kirkkojärvi-Uusikylä road trucks in 200 metre intervals heading to Yläuuksu. At Uusikylä a column of 30 trucks heading to Yläuuksu. Three kilometres north-west of Uusikylä a column of 60–70 trucks at rest.

The south-western shore of Karkunlampi lake full of aircraft in two rows, much over 50. Bombed with four aircraft (BL-115, 106, 119 and 118) from 700 metres. Each plane had 2x100kg, 6x50kg, 2x12,5kg and 2x15kg incendiaries. The bombs hit exceptionally well. After the attack several fighters appeared and the anti-aircraft fire was dense.

The Gulf of Finland had now become fully frozen and the submarine hunting turned into reconnoitring of motorized sleighs and movements of the infantry. Harassment bombing went on as before. On the Soviet side, 49 IAP claimed one Fokker D.XXI and two Fokker C.Xs shot down, and 38 IAP claimed one Fokker D.XXI in central Finland. 21 DBAP claimed four Fokker D.XXIs north-east of Lake Ladoga.

Since LeR 2 units were now spread all over southern Finland, the commander of the air defences ordered the regiment to transfer the headquarters to Selänpää, for better communication connections. The move was made on 21 January. That day, ten long-nose Blenheims also arrived at Luonetjärvi as new equipment for LLv 46. Simultaneously, the remaining five short-nose Blenheims were transferred to LLv 44, which became the only front line squadron of the regiment, as LLv 46 took up an extensive training programme for a month.

On 22 January, LLv 10 carried out the next squadron bombing, when seven aircraft dive-bombed the air base on the ice of Lake Karkunlampi on the east coast of Lake Ladoga. The inaccurate information of the location of the aircraft lines caused the bombs to miss just by one or two lengths of the aircraft in front of them, but possibly broke the ice. 49 IAP claimed one Fokker D.XXI and one biplane shot down.

In Lapland on 23 January, F 19 Gladiators flew combat air patrols over the front, tasked with preventing Soviet fighters from strafing. In the ensuing combat, one Gladiator was shot down. That day in Lapland, 145 IAP claimed one reconnaissance biplane shot down. The next day only nocturnal harassment bombings of LeR 1 could be accomplished. On 25 January, Capt. Birger Gabrielsson was appointed to command LLv 10, while, on 26 January, LLv 10 lost one Fokker C.X (FK-81), including the crew of two, on a reconnaissance mission

1Lt Per Sovelius was the deputy leader of 4/LLv 24, since Maj. Magnusson also preferred to lead a flight, in addition to the whole squadron. Sovelius is standing here in front of his Fokker FR-92 'black 5' in January 1940. He scored all of his eight Winter War victories flying this particular plane.

Stenbäck: bombing the ice airfields, 20 January 1940

Only a 1km-wide isthmus separated the small lake of Karkunlampi from the shore in the middle of northeast Lake Ladoga. On 19 January 1940, Blenheim BL-106 of LLv 46 was returning from a reconnaissance mission along the north coast of Lake Ladoga, observing over 50 aircraft parked on the ice in two irregular lines on the southwest shore of Karkunlanpi. It had already dropped most of the bombs in earlier harassment targets and had only four 12.5 kg small bombs left, releasing them from 1500m and hitting the lines directly, which consisted of I-15bis, I-16 and R-5 aircraft.

The following morning, LLv 44 sent four Blenheims led by the squadron CO Maj. Erik Stenbäck to attack Karkunlampi. The Blenheims flew low over Lake Ladoga undetected and, at 0905hrs, released the bombs on the lines of enemy planes from 700m altitude. All bombs were seen to hit the planes. Then, Russian fighters – already in the air – appeared on the scene. However, the greater speed of the Blenheims took them out of range of the fighters, in the escape along the north coast of Lake Ladoga to the northwest towards the Finnish lines. In light of this success, LLv 10 attempted on 22 January 1940 to dive-bomb Karkunlampi ice base with seven Fokker C.X planes. There were plenty of aircraft, but not in exactly the same position and the dive-bombing failed, with bombs hitting the ice 10–15m in front of the planes, possibly breaking the ice.

Reconnaissance squadron LLv 14 was only partly equipped with the Fokker C.X, flying early in the conflict with the obsolete Fokker C.V aircraft. Here is FO-68 of 3/LLv 14 photographed at Räisälä in January 1940. It wears a practical (but then quite rare) winter camouflage, which was done by a mixture of chalk and casein glue. The C.V was still suited for nocturnal harassment bombings of enemy camps and troops.

north of Lake Ladoga. That day, 49 IAP also claimed one Fokker C.X shot down north of Lake Ladoga. Fog and low cloud on 27 January prevented all but one maritime reconnaissance mission by LLv 36.

Though up till now the Soviet fighters had shot down only two Fokkers, there had been a number of close calls. On 28 January, LeR 2 commander Lt Col. Richard Lorentz issued a firm ban on searching out and engaging enemy fighters — only the bombers were to be attacked. The Fokker D.XXI was no match for the much more manoeuvrable Polikarpov I-153s and I-16s, which also possessed huge numerical superiority.

On 29 January, several Soviet vessels were observed arriving at Saunasaari on the southwestern coast of Lake Ladoga. Six dive-bombers of LLv 10 attacked two larger vessels that were anchored there. The bomb rows crossed both vessels damaging both. The extremely sharp and accurate anti-aircraft fire shot down one C.X and ripped the landing gear off another. The bombing report said:

Aircraft and crews: FL-88 1Lt Pietarinen and Sgt Kirjavainen, FK-111 2Lt Nenonen and 2Lt Roschier, FK-89 WO Hämelä and 1Lt Bärlund, FK-108 1Lt Nurminen and Cpl Laine, FK-86 SSgt Louko and 2Lt Rahko and FK-85 Sgt Rekola and Sgt Peltonen. Take-off at 1555hrs and meeting the escort of six Fokker D.XXIs above Käkisalmi at 1605hrs. Dive-bombing at 1615hrs from 900 metres. Bombs each plane 2x 100kg and 8x 12.5kg, release at 0.2 second intervals.

Results: Crew 1: Large bombs on or just next to the large vessel, small bombs on both sides of the vessel. Crew 2: Enemy flak hit at the beginning of the dive and the plane caught fire crashing on the ice. Crew 3: Large bombs were stuck as the flak hit tore the landing gear away, small bombs on both sides of the vessel. Emergency landing of a forward landing strip with no additional damage. Crew 4. Went into a back dive and missed to release the bombs. Due to heavy flak could not repeat the dive, landing with the bombs in the forward landing strip. Crew 5: All but one of the small bombs on or just next to the icebreakers. Five shrapnel holes. Crew 6: As the previous crew. Six shrapnel holes. The anti-aircraft artillery shot a cover on the target and the fire was very fierce and accurate. One heavy AA, four light AA and possible another heavy AA batteries were observed.

Recent research shows that minesweeper No. 32 was sunk and No. 34 severely damaged, both vessels belonging to the Lake Ladoga Naval Detachment.

On the Karelian Isthmus, the Russian artillery was firing with the aid of Polikarpov R-5 spotting aircraft. The Karelian Army commander contacted LeR 2 commander requesting a stop be put to this, and 1Lt Jorma Karhunen of LLv 24 told how the job was done:

At 1455hrs I got an order to take off with four Fokkers to Summa, either to drive away or destroy two artillery fire-control R-5 planes. Five minutes later the Fokker swarm speeded on the ice and took off. WO Yrjö Turkka was my wingman in the lead pair while 2Lt Olli Mustonen headed the other pair with Sgt Tauno Kaarma as wingman.

I plotted the battle plan, which had to be foolproof. The enemy planes were called off as soon as a smallest hint of arriving Finns was received. When the Finns were gone they popped up again. I decided to fool the airspace control of the enemy properly.

We flew along the west coast of Viipurinlahti at the cloud line on 2,000 metres. We continued to the south and at Koivisto we turned towards Summa. I took the swarm inside the clouds. When approaching Summa I pulled my FR-80 out of the cloud just to make sure that the 'patients' were still there. There they circled distributing instructions to the artillery. A way to go and I returned inside the clouds. Three minutes took a long time, but I controlled myself. Then we bounced out of the clouds.

One R-5 was conveniently below the lead pair. We attacked together with 'Daddy' Turkka and fired simultaneously from up ahead and behind. In a moment the wings collapsed together after the fuselage burst into fire. The flaming ball of fire came down between the lines. Then we all fired at the other R-5 and it crashed beyond the lines. The job was done.

We also managed to get unhurt out of the fierce anti-aircraft fire back to the own side, which as such was a miracle.

The fighter defence of the State Aircraft Factory was organized by test pilots, occasionally assisted by front line pilots picking up repaired aircraft. An example occurred this afternoon, as reported by 2Lt Olli Puhakka, a member of LLv 26 on assignment to LLv 24, showing exceptional gunnery skills:

At 1600hrs. After an interception with 1Lt Visapää we were about to land at Tampere airfield. He was about 200 metres ahead of me and almost above the runway, when we observed a large twin-engined aircraft flying a transverse course to us.

1Lt Visapää fired instantly from the side, but was left behind me in the climbing turn while I remained 500–700 metres behind the enemy plane. In the chase I noticed that the distance rather increased than the opposite. I started to fire short bursts. The first one went below. Judged by the cannon shell explosions, I seemed to hit with the second burst around the port engine and the third burst hit the starboard side.

Probably either engine got damaged, because I instantly caught the plane, but now the guns did not work anymore. After a few dives towards the plane, I left it between Lempäälä and Viiala assuming that 1Lt Visapää on my starboard side would attack it, but he had lost it in a cloud almost simultaneously.

I assume that the shooting was seen by 1Lt Itävuori and 1Lt Visapää. The forced-landed plane was probably taken into custody by T-LentoR 2, so information from there would tell whether the landing was caused by cannon shells or MG bullets, the latter could also have been fired by 1Lt Visapää.

I flew FR-76 equipped with a 20mm cannon in each wing, but only the other one was working. I used all 18 rounds in the drum. The fuselage MGs had fired about 60–70 rounds, when the synchronizing gear broke down.

This aircraft was an Ilyushin DB-3M of 53 DBAP and the crew was captured after a forced landing at Urjala. The cannon hits gave the credit of the downing to Puhakka.

30 January was a sad day for LLv 24. The 2nd Flight leader, 1Lt Jaakko Vuorela (flying FR-78), crashed in poor weather at Ruokolahti and was killed. 1Lt Leo Ahola took over the unit, forming Detachment Ahola and 1Lt Jorma Karhunen now headed the 2nd Flight. The Fokkers claimed one SB bomber shot down at Virolahti.

Saunasaari, 29 January 1940

Finnish coast surveillance observed a number of vessels landing at Saunasaari pier, on the south-west coast of Lake Ladoga, including what was thought to be an icebreaker and a transport ship. LLv 10 was ordered to attack on the 29 January 1940 with six Fokker C.X dive-bombers led by 1Lt Aimo Pietarinen. Bombs were released from 900m at 1615hrs which hit both vessels, but fierce Soviet flak struck one Fokker at the start of its dive which crashed into flames on the ice. Another was damaged by flak swiping the skis away. The plane managed to make a successful forced landing and the other four escaped unharmed. Modern research shows that sweeper No. 32 was sunk and sweeper No. 34 was badly damaged, both vessels belonging to the Lake Ladoga Naval Detachment.

LAKE LADOGA

EVENTS

4. The first section dives down and releases bombs at 900m.

5. Soviet flak strikes FK-111 and it crashes on the ice.

6. The second section approaches from the west.

7. Minesweeper No. 32 is sunk.

8. Minesweeper No. 34 is badly damaged.

9. Both sections exit.

light flak

heavy flak

Three fighter pilots of 4/LLv 24 at the cockpit of a Fokker D.XXI. In the cockpit is the flight deputy leader, 1Lt Per Sovelius, above 2Lt Olli Mustonen and, at the step, 2Lt Iikka Törrönen. Törrönen was wearing common mittens made of dog fur, which were quite useful at temperatures of often minus 30 and, on occasion, minus 40 degrees centigrade.

On the last day of the month, LLv 10 returned to Lappeenranta, after having lost three aircraft in missions north of Lake Ladoga. At the end of the month there were now 28 serviceable Fokkers in LLv 24, when ten 'hired' pilots returned to their original unit Lentolaivue 26, which had just began receiving Gloster Gladiators. January's score for the Fokkers still showed 34 enemy aircraft shot down.

February 1940

By February, the Soviet Union had concentrated two armies in the Karelian Isthmus. The northwestern Front was occupied by the 7th Army on the western side and the 13th Army on the eastern, altogether encompassing 23 divisions of infantry, six armoured brigades and two detached armoured battalions. The task was to break through the Finnish defences and to advance to Helsinki. Protecting the army group were 30 aviation regiments and the Baltic Fleet air forces, totalling just over 2,000 aircraft in all.

After a standstill at the fronts, the Soviet Union launched the second phase of the offensive on 1 February, on the Karelian Isthmus. Other fronts were left as they were, as all strength was concentrated here for a breakthrough. The bomber offensive against Finland was switched to immediate support of the attack and large fighter formations started patrolling over the front and immediate rear.

At noon, in bright daylight, LLv 12 photographed the front on the Karelian Isthmus. SSgt Marttila and Sgt Salminen manned FK-105 and the clear pictures revealed the spearhead of the Russian attack. Four Fokker fighters of LLv 24 acted as an escort. FR-115 was shot down, killing 2Lt Tapani Harmaja, while protecting the photo-reconnaissance plane from an attack by about 40 enemy fighters. Two fighters were claimed by 7 IAP.

On 2 February 1940, LLv 24 claimed two SB and one DB-3 bombers on the Karelian Isthmus. WO Viktor Pyötsiä reported the following:

At 1140hrs. Five plane SB formation. I attacked the outmost right flank plane, of which the port engine caught instantly fire. The formation reduced the speed, so my victim could stay with it for a while. I then shot at the right flank plane when thick smoke came out of its starboard engine.

My guns ceased to fire. I saw a total of 41 SB bombers coming from south over Sortavala and north of it turned east to Kitelä. The bombers flew at 2,000–3,000m altitude in groups of 5–9 planes and 1–2 kilometres apart. My victim was found at Hämekoski as a wreck. My plane was FR-110.

LLv 24 also lost FR-81 and Danish volunteer, 1Lt Frits Rasmussen, to 25 IAP fighters. Detachment Ahola flew to Turku on the southwest coast in protection of the main port, and to prevent Soviet forces flying northbound along the west coast.

After two weeks of familiarization flights, LLv 26 opened the score on this day when 1Lt Paavo Berg fought against six I-153s of 38 IAP, shooting down one on a transfer flight en route to the base. His combat report stated:

At 1040hrs I saw at 2,000m altitude, myself at 3,000m, six aircraft arriving from south, believing that these were SB bombers. I commenced the attack from behind. Already during the dive I observed that these were of a strange type and probably fighters. I approached from behind and started shooting, when both 3-plane patrols scattered and when looking back I saw three similar planes diving towards me. I dodged them and noticed entering in a curve battle with them.

At the beginning it was easy, when there were several planes, but in the end when there were only three left, began the dodging and shooting feel difficult, as there was always one behind my tail. I got then one pouring smoke and it departed towards Tammisaari. After one evasion I observed to be alone and the remaining two enemies were flying southwards. I did not go for a chase, but instead flew circles as I suspected a surprise from behind.

According to the local air surveillance boss there were about 20 enemy planes. One had landed on the ice between Bromarv and Petu and was in a pretty good shape. The planes had similar speed and agility as the I-16. My plane was GL-263.

Later, SSgt Oiva Tuominen of 2/LLv 26 chased two SBs and six I-16s to the Gulf of Finland sending one fighter down at Kotka and another near the island of Suursaari. He recounted the event as follows:

At 1520–1615hrs. Between Inkeroinen and Elimäki I caught two SBs and six I-16s, but could not attack the bombers as the fighters targeted me. Then I got to fire on the first I-16 from straight ahead, when the plane went into a spin and disappeared from my sight.

When shooting at the second fighter the others went out of my sight. I saw one flying towards Kotka. I caught it outside Kotka and fired from straight behind, when it landed on the ice. When the pilot tried to escape I shot him on the ice.

A Gloster Gladiator of LLv 26 with engine running in front of a field servicing hangar, at Joutseno in February 1940. While waiting for their actual equipment – Italian Fiat G.50 fighters – to arrive, LLv 26 flew with their temporary Gladiators for six weeks, claiming 34 enemy aircraft shot down.

Then one I-16 got behind me, fired and turned to the sea. While it curved I caught it at the north tip of Suursaari, fired and it crashed on the ice.

The speed of the I-16 did not appear to be so great because with full throttle I caught it quite easy, starting from 1,000m distance. I-16 is not so agile as the Gladiator. The first I-16 was on wheels, gear in. My plane GL-258 was intact.

That day, 25 IAP claimed 11 Fokker D.XXIs and one two-seat fighter shot down. Additionally, 38 IAP claimed two aircraft destroyed and 7 DBAP one Fokker D.XXI. 57 AP, KBF claimed one Fokker over the Gulf of Finland.

On 3 February, 1Lt Jorma Sarvanto of LLv 24 claimed his tenth kill, shooting down an Ilyushin DB-3M bomber of 51 DBAP at Nuijamaa in southeastern Finland. Another victor was the squadron CO Maj. Gustaf Magnusson:

At 1510hrs. I met about 10km north of Joutseno 18 DB-3 bombers. I attacked the plane on the extreme right wing. The fuselage guns jammed and only the wing guns fired. I shot the plane's port engine into fire. The wreck was found 3km south-west of Joutseno.

Then I attacked another bomber, but only the left-wing gun was functioning. The port engine poured smoke, but the plane continued to fly in the formation. Due to the gun jamming I spent only 350 rounds. My plane was FR-92.

In the west four Fokkers took three DB-3 bombers of 10 ABr, KBF (Aviation Brigade, Baltic Fleet air forces) completely by surprise, and sent them all down in Turku archipelago, with 2Lt Pekka Kokko claiming a double. That day, 42 DBAP claimed four fighters over central Finland.

Airmen of 1/LLv 14 at Kaukola forward base in February 1940. From left: three unknown, MSgt O. Kajutti, 1Lt E. Honkanen, flight leader 1Lt M. Eskola, 2Lt P. Kahla, Sgt M. Perälä, MSgt J. Harju and three unknown. Later, in the Continuation War, Kahla became the first observer to win the Mannerheim Cross. LLv 14 operated most of the time over the eastern Karelian Isthmus, providing good reconnaissance information for the land forces.

On 4 February, one DB-3 was shot down over the sea southwest of Turku and the Russians became cautious in this direction. The sudden appearance of a Finnish fighter unit was not expected this far west. The next day on the Karelian Isthmus, the Soviet 7th Army tried again to get through the Mannerheim Line, in vain. Otherwise, the poor weather did not allow flying.

On 6 February, poor weather cancelled missions to the front. In the west, LLv 28, which had received the first of 30 Morane-Saulnier M.S. 406 fighters from France, performed the first combat mission from Säkylä, flying in the defence of Turku and other southwestern ports. The poor weather then continued, with only a few routine reconnaissance and harassment bombing missions flown on 7 February, and on 8 February most of the missions to the front were aborted.

On 9 February, the Fokkers of LLv 24 took off for 31 interception sorties to the front at the Karelian Isthmus and claimed two R-5s shot down. Future 22-victory ace, Sgt Eero Kinnunen claimed one and wrote in the combat report:

SSgt Lauri Nissinen of 3/LLv 24 in February 1940. He shot down five aircraft flying FR-98, becoming an ace in the Winter War. Later, in the Continuation War, Nissinen took the cadet courses and became a regular officer. In the later conflict, he added 28 planes to his score and was a Mannerheim Cross winner.

At 1130hrs. I attacked from behind and above a solitary R-5. At this point I was able to fire when almost colliding with it, before it took evasive action, a 180-degree turn. I turned after it, but when it observed me behind its tail, it turned the nose towards me. We flew now from opposite directions both shooting. At this point it began to smoke and when passing it went into a 45-degree dive. I turned after it and shot from straight behind from 50 metres. Then it caught fire and crashed on the ground.

I used 1,200 rounds. To me it seemed to catch the fire in the middle of the upper wing. My plane was FR-109.

That day, 10 ABr, KBF claimed one Fokker shot down in southwestern Finland.

On 10 February, 4/LLv 24 attacked a large bomber formation over Lappeenranta, but the equally numerous fighter escort handled the situation and shot down one Fokker, FR-102, wounding MSgt Väinö Ikonen. Big claims were now history for the Fokker pilots, as the daily scores were three bombers at the most. Losses also started to accumulate.

The Soviet commenced a new attack on the Karelian Isthmus at Summa sector on 11 February, which would lead into a crack in the main defence line three days later. On the 11th, three Gladiators of LLv 26 fought with 15 I-16s north of Lake Ladoga and claimed one destroyed. The first Fiat G.50 arrived to LLv 26 at Utti. Another 13 more were to follow during the course of the month.

On 12 February, LeR 1 flew the usual reconnaissance missions. LLv 12 was reorganized and the 1st Flight was formed into a fighter unit equipped with Gladiators. The other two flights flew still the Fokker C.X and the reconnaissance report of this day read:

At 1800–2015hrs. Plane FK-92 Capt. Maunula and MSgt Tiukkanen. Altitude 1,000–4,000 metres. Observations:

On the road from Lähde to Kaukjärvi airfield, campfires on both sides of the road, up to the crossroad between Kaukjärvi artillery camp and Perkjärvi station. Judging from this the depth of enemy troops extended at least to the crossroad level.

On the road from Summankylä and Kaukjärvi artillery camp plenty of campfires. On the road from Koskikylä via Perkjärvi station to Liikola heavy truck traffic to north. On the road

Gladiators of 2/LLv 26 at Mensuvaara in February 1940. Closest is GL-255, which SSgt Oiva Tuominen was flying on 13 February, when he claimed three whole and one shared SB bombers plus one I-15bis fighter shot down on a single mission, making him the first Gladiator ace. Early in the Continuation War, Tuominen became the first air arm Mannerheim Cross winner and ended the war with 47 air victories. At right is GL-253.

between Liikola and Kantelejärvi solitary trucks, likewise between Liikola and Mustamäki. On the road between Mustamäki and Vammneljärvi solitary trucks.

On the road between Vammelsuu and Uusikirkko a continuous column of trucks to north. Some lights at the end of the south-east end of Riskjärvi. On the road between Kantelejärvi station and Uusikirkko a continuous truck column towards Uusikirkko. On the road from Uusikirkko via Kiskola to Kaukjärvi artillery camp continuous truck traffic to north, likewise from Uusikirkko via Halila to Iivanala.

At Kiskola 6–8 lights, at Siparila 10 lights, at Kaukjärvi over ten lights, south of Leppäniemi 4–5 lights, 1km east of Hyväjärvi a few lights.

On the road between Lounatjoki and Uiskola heavy truck traffic to west. On the road between Putru saw mill and Halilanjärvi 6-8 trucks at the south end. On the road from Munalampi to Piispala 10–12 trucks heading to Piispala.

On the coast road from Ino via Seivästö to Lautaranta no traffic. Neither on the southern railway. No bombs carried.

A total of seven searchlights in function between Kaukjärvi and Perkjärvi stations. 14 searchlights in function in Kantelejärvi-Raivola-Halilanjärvi terrain. Especially intense flak fire from area between Kaukjärvi and Perkjärvi stations. 5,000 leaflets dropped between Summa and the main railway, 2,000 leaflets between Muolaanjärvi and the main railway and 3,000 leaflets between Halilanjärvi and Kaukjärvi.

A pair of Gladiators of LLv 26 intercepted eight SB bombers of 18 SBAP north of Lake Ladoga and sent one down. It was claimed by Danish volunteer 1Lt Carl Kalmberg.

On 13 February, the 1st Flight of LLv 14 was also equipped with Gladiators, becoming a fighter outfit. LLv 24 flew 71 sorties, but failed to gain any results in combat. Six Gladiators of LLv 26 engaged in combat with I-153s north of Lake Ladoga when nine SBs of 39 SBAP arrived on the spot, simultaneously with WO Lauri Lautamäki's pair, which, undisturbed, attacked the bombers, shooting four down in a quick succession. Future 47-victory ace and Mannerheim Cross recipient, SSgt Oiva Tuominen reported the clash thus:

At 1400–1530hrs. When I was patrolling with WO Lautamäki in Jänisjärvi station area, I noticed nine SBs arriving east of Suojärvi and heading west. I signalled WO Lautamäki and turned towards the enemy planes. The enemy formation banked to east and east of Soanjoki I caught them and shot the port wing aircraft into fire. It crashed in the woods. So did the next one after a minute. And the third crashed into a small pond.

Then nine more bombers arrived from Loimola direction joining the others. At first I thought they were fighters as the distance grew a little, but I caught them over Kivijärvi and shot at the starboard wing aircraft. When I fired the second burst it crashed in flames to the north bank of Kivijärvi lake.

At the same time an I-15 took off from the ice, I shot it immediately down at the edge of the forest, where it crashed in fire. My fighter had two bullet holes in the wings fired from the ground. My plane was GL-255.

SSgt Tuominen's share was three and a half SB bombers, plus a solitary I-15, and thus he became the first Gladiator ace. Other Gladiators then attacked the bombers and claimed another two destroyed. On the Soviet side, 49 IAP claimed two Gladiators and one Fokker D.XXI shot down, in two combats.

On 14 February, the 7th Army forced the Finnish infantry to withdraw 4km from the main defensive line. LeR 1 began daylight reconnaissance missions after having received Gladiators, which made precise observation of the enemy's ground movements possible. Regular nocturnal missions and harassment bombing continued. LLv 24 flew 69 sorties, protecting troop transfers on the way to Karelian Isthmus in order to repel the 7th Army. Two bombers of 19-aircraft strong 48 SBAP were shot down near Lappeenranta. That day, 42 DBAP claimed one fighter shot down.

Since Lappeenranta air base was under continuous Russian air attacks, LLv 10 flew to Taipalsaari and the next day, on 15 February, was tasked to support the Karelian Isthmus army groupings holding the enemy outside of Viipuri. That day the fighters of LeR 2 claimed two DB-3 bombers and one R-5 light bomber shot down.

On 16 February, LeR 1 continuously reconnoitred the spearhead of the Russian advance. At noon LLv 12 sent 2Lt Ossi Marttila to scout with a Gladiator. His report said briefly:

> My plane GL-272, height 200 metres. Observations: Main force heading from Kämärä station westwards, first troops at the bend of Suurjoki river consisting of 10 tanks and 15 vehicles of motorized troops. Then another 10 tanks and 5 vehicles. Three tanks towards Kämärä village, two kilometres away. Lehtola-Kämärä road full of tanks and motorized troops, firing at the aircraft.

The tail of Blenheim BL-117 in February 1940. This bomber was assigned to 1/LLv 44 pilot WO Viljo Salminen. The rudder wears one of very few individual markings on any Finnish Air Force aircraft at that time. Salminen became the first bomber command member to receive the Mannerheim Cross, later in the Continuation War.

That day, LLv 24 flew 47 sorties and LLv 26 claimed one I-16 shot down, while 7 IAP claimed one fighter shot down.

On 17 February, LeR 1 squadron continued nocturnal harassment bombing of enemy groupings in addition to routine reconnaissance missions. The main target of Soviet bombers was on several occasions Kouvola, an important railway and road junction. LLv 24 managed to scatter two 30-strong bomber formations over the immediate rear of the Karelian Isthmus front. In 26 combats, three bombers were shot down. Future 32-victory ace and Mannerheim Cross recipient, SSgt Lauri Nissinen related:

> At 1530hrs. I saw with Cpl Vahvelainen seven SBs escorted by twenty fighters about 700m behind them at 4,000m altitude. The enemy planes went north of Turku heading towards south-east. We climbed to 6,000m above the bombers and then I signaled for the attack.
>
> We dived in front of the fighters under the bombers and then attacked from below and behind. The SBs were in two layers, five higher and two lower. I attacked the lower left plane

shooting from 200m to 30m, when the starboard engine caught fire and the landing gear dropped down. Because of the firing of the fighters I was forced to break off by a semi-roll to a vertical dive. The fighters did not follow.

The fighter escort flew too far behind the bombers and could not make it to help the bombers. My plane was FR-98.

Based in southwestern Finland in protection of vital ports, LLv 28 had only two weeks to become acquainted with the French fighter plan, the Morane. In the afternoon, the Moranes drew the first blood. 1Lt Tuomo Hyrkki's pair engaged a lone DB-3 bomber of 53 DBAP claiming it destroyed. Hyrkki reported it thus:

At 1410–1515hrs. Flying at 3,500m altitude I observed above Rauma a solitary bomber flying southwards 1,000m lower than me. I dived after it and recognized as a DB-3. First I shot the gunner from below and behind and continued to the left engine. When I did not get it into fire, I pulled steeply up from below and gave a burst to the cockpit, when from the right side of the pilot flashed a sharp flame. Soon after this the whole fuselage was on fire. The bomber exploded mid-air and fell in three large pieces on the ice south-west of Korppoo. The pilot bailed out using his parachute.

Each time when I got closer than 50m, the bomber pilot pulled up his plane by shutting the throttle and then banking to either side. I got the impression that the pilot intended to cause a crash after noting that escaping was not possible. My plane was MS-301.

That day, 25 IAP claimed three Fokker D.XXIs and 38 IAP another two. 54 IAB claimed two Bulldogs. 10 ABr, KBF claimed two Fokkers in southwestern Finland.

On 18 February, LeR 1 flew 33 nocturnal bombing sorties to Summa sector attacking columns and camps. LLv 12 took a Gladiator patrol for a daylight reconnaissance mission, as told by future Mannerheim Cross winner Capt. Auvo Maunula:

At 1455–1540hrs. Altitude 1,000–3,000 metres. Planes GL-270 Capt. Maunula, GL-271 2Lt Marttila and GL-272 MSgt Tiukkanen. Observations:

On the road between Johannes and Yläkylä one 3.5km long column, from Vahtola crossing to east, heading west. Then for 3km road empty, whereafter a solid column to Ylikylä, infantry, trucks and tanks. Then onwards the same to the north end of Suursuo.

On the road between Munasuo and Kämärä station, a solid column to east. On the road between Huumola and Näykkijärvi a scarse column to east. On the road between Huumola and Metsäkylä a solid column from Metsäkylä to Sydänmaanniitty. On the road between Kämärä and Kämärä station a few tanks.

No flak encountered and visibility was good.

That day, over 300 Soviet aircraft bombed Viipuri. LLv 24 flew 65 interception sorties, claiming three bombers shot down. Sgt Eero Kinnunen got one, reporting the following:

At 0905hrs. Our flight attacked a twelve-plane enemy bomber formation. For a while I remained as the top cover because I saw five I-15 fighters behind and above a little further away. When the fighters turned to east, I attacked and got behind one SB, I fired from straight behind from 30–50 metres, first to the fuselage and then to the engines, the port one caught fire and the starboard one began to smoke.

The enemy planes changed the flight path 10–15 degrees to both sides, opening and closing the throttle. Nobody bailed out. I used 1,200 rounds because only three guns worked. My plane was FR-109.

Detachment Siiriäinen of LLv 26 destroyed two 54 SBAP bombers out of 40, near Kouvola. The victories were credited to 1Lt Paavo Berg, who reported it thus:

At 1115–1145hrs. I met south of Kouvola an SB formation consisting of 40 bombers. I attacked the plane at the extreme right wing, which started to pour black and white smoke.

I received then fire from the side and dodged (probably I-153). In this manoeuvre I got in the middle of a 9-plane SB formation, of which I managed to shoot the left engine of one bomber into smoke. I shot also at others at close range, but without visual effect. The defensive fire was so dense that I evaded downwards, putting me behind the SB formation again.

There was one plane already smoking and was left behind. I managed to cut the curve of the SB formation and caught it easily. The machine-guns had stopped working and I stayed to wait for the next plane. When it came close I saw that the left engine had stopped and the crew was alive because they were shooting at me. Since the guns stayed jammed I returned to the base.

According to the air surveillance report, one smoking plane hit the forest south of Kouvola and one on fire northeast of Kouvola. The SB planes dodged firing by making stairs up and down. My plane GL-264 had twelve bullet holes.

Enemy fighters managed to send down Blenheim BL-113 of LLv 44, which was performing a photo-reconnaissance mission north of Lake Ladoga. Only the pilot bailed out.

25 IAP claimed two Fokker D.XXIs and one bomber and 49 IAP claimed a Blenheim that day. Forty SBs of 54 SBAP escorted by 12 fighters of 149 IAP had attacked Kouvola, with the bombs dropped at 1152–1159hrs. Three SBs were damaged by heavy anti-aircraft machine-gun fire. Furthermore, 3 and 5 escadrilles were attacked over the target by five Bulldogs and nine Fokker D.XXI. In the following combat, the gunners claimed two Bulldogs, while their own losses were limited to two damaged SBs: one piloted by Lt V. V. Butrim received 22 bullet holes, mainly in the left wing and navigator's cockpit, and landed safely at the own airfield, while the second SB flown by Lt N. I. Ivanov was forced to land at Kotly airfield, with navigator Lt A. A. Smirnov being wounded in his right hand.

Gladiators of 1/LLv 26 at Ruokolahti in February 1940. Nearest is GL-262, which was shot down on 29 February, killing 1Lt Aimo Halme. Next is GL-254, which was shot down on 25 February, killing 1Lt Pentti Tevä. The lack of armour and self-sealing fuel tanks were the main reasons for the serious losses.

Four pilots of 3/LLv 24 at Ruokolahti in February 1940. From left: flight leader Capt. Eino Luukkanen, Sgt Jalo Dahl, MSgt Ilmari Juutilainen and Sgt Martti Alho. Of these men, Juutilainen was to become the top scorer in the Continuation War, with 94 air victories and a double Mannerheim Cross winner. The latter being awarded only to four soldiers, Juutilainen being the first.

I-153 escort fighters of 149 IAP reported combat with two Fokker D.XXIs and four Bulldogs to the south of target, and claimed three victories: Maj. Plygunov one Bulldog, Maj. Kuldin one Fokker D.XXI, and Lt. Litvinenko one Fokker D.XXI. Near the target the fighters met heavy anti-aircraft fire, Lt Litvinenko's I-153 receiving 36 holes from the close explosion of a shell. Nevertheless, it safely landed at its own airfield.

On 19 February, LeR 1 carried out 30 nocturnal bombing missions on the Karelian Isthmus, targeting the Huumola and Summa areas.

Large formations of bombers escorted by numerous fighters flew over the Karelian Isthmus. LLv 24 took off for 60 interception missions and claimed two bombers destroyed, while 25 I AP fighters shot down Danish volunteer 1Lt Erhard Frijs in FR-80 near Käkisalmi, killing him in the attack.

Three Gladiators of LLv 26 engaged several fighters during a chase of a 32-strong bomber formation. Two I-153s were claimed shot down. That same day, LeR 4 also flew the first sortie to the Karelian Isthmus. One Blenheim photographed the traffic on route Kuolemanjärvi-Raivola-Terijoki. LeR 4 also photographed the islands of Suursaari, Tytärsaari and Seiskari in the Gulf of Finland.

For the Soviets, 25 IAP claimed six Fokker D.XXIs shot down and 7 IAP one more fighter. 1AP, KBF claimed six Fokkers shot down in Lappeenranta area.

On 20 February, the Soviet 7th Army broke through the intermediary line on the Karelian Isthmus, but the next day the advance was temporarily stopped. LeR 1 bombed the spearhead of the Soviet attack in 21 sorties. LLv 24 received 480 observations of Soviet bombers and climbed for 59 interception sorties. They failed to prevent the bombardment of Elisenvaara railway junction, when the transfer of a division to the Karelian Isthmus was delayed.

This day saw the second Gladiator ace. 1Lt Berg of LLv 26 took off to attack 30 SB bombers of 6 DBAP with Kouvola as the target. Flying GL-280, he sent one down, but was in turn shot into flames by the defensive fire and bailed out, suffering burns. LLv 28 shot down two bombers out of six which were approaching to bomb the port of Rauma. Later, one Morane chased nine bombers of 53 SBAP towards Estonia. Future Mannerheim Cross winner 1Lt Veikko Karu caught the formation just at the Estonian coastline and sent down two, as his report highlights:

At 1415–1530hrs. I was on an interception mission with two Moranes in Kokemäki area flying at 3,000m. When I observed a 9-plane enemy formation it was 25–30km from me and 3,000-4,000m higher. I caught the enemy very slowly, even when flying at full throttle (and using a few times the additional boost). When approaching the Estonian coast and about to engage the enemy formation, I observed an enemy fighter formation climbing towards me, first six planes 1,000-2,000m below me and under this a similar detachment.

I attacked first the bomber at the extreme right wing and then moved on to the next. I attacked from behind and below, staying constantly under the cover of the tail. The enemy planes caught fire easily after shooting at close range (maybe 20–30m) three short bursts, making my attack to last just a moment. After the attack on these two bombers I saw the enemy fighters threateningly close behind my tail.

I don't remember if the enemy fighters fired at me, but anyway they were very close, so I thought that it was best to quit and took a dive via a half-roll. The combat occurred at

7,500m. During the vertical dive I took first a 180-degree aileron turn and before levelling a second. I began the pull up at 2,000m. My plane seemed to hold well that heavy dive. I did not observe any kind of vibrations in the wings or tail. I saw no enemy fighter anywhere. Just to be sure I flew with full throttle close to the Finnish coast.

I came to the conclusion that my attack must have come as a total surprise, because I did not observe any counter fire from the bombers nor did I observe any evasive actions for defence. Though I did not pay much attention to this matter as I would not have had time to fire at the gunners first. Very likely the condensation stream left by the bombers had covered my approach.

I had to stay above 5,000m a fair half hour, of which time 15–20 minutes above 7,000m without oxygen equipment. My condition was not pleasant, but not so bad that I would have aborted the attack at the bombers. In my opinion experience is quite significant in flying at higher altitudes. During the previous week I had frequently been up to 6,000m without oxygen gear during interception missions, so this case did not feel more unpleasant. My plane was MS-321.

On that same day, LeR 4 photographed the islands of Suursaari, Tytärsaari and Seiskari in the Gulf of Finland and the naval and air base at Paldiski. 7 IAP claimed six fighters in two encounters and 54 IAB three Gamecocks. 53 DBAP claimed four fighters shot down. 10 ABr, KBF claimed three fighters shot down in south-western Finland.

On 21 February, the breakthrough on the western Karelian Isthmus was repelled. Aerial reconnaissance by LeR 1 provided vital information for the Finnish responses. Many Finnish fighter bases and forward landing grounds came under almost continuous attack from patrolling Soviet fighters. LLv 24 claimed two bombers and two fighters shot down in the encounters. In Lapland, a pair of Gladiators of F 19 engaged a DB squadron in the vicinity of Rovaniemi and sent one down, damaging another. From this point on, Lapland would no longer be a target of air raids.

On 22 February, LeR 4 long-range reconnaissance planes made observations confirming that, in the Suomussalmi and Kuhmo directions, the Soviet advance remained at a standstill. F 19 in Lapland had received another Hart light bomber and kept on nocturnal harassment bombings of Soviet campsites. On the right flank on the Karelian Isthmus front, Finnish troops began their withdrawal from Koivisto island on 23 February. LLv 24 was asked to protect the operation, but poor weather prevented all flying. Likewise, all-day dense fog on 24 February meant no flying.

On 25 February, LeR 1 squadrons continued nocturnal nuisance attacks against Soviet troop concentration and camp areas. This day proved costly for both parties on the Karelian Isthmus. LLv 26 sent three Gladiators to drive off nine R-5 artillery spotting planes, escorted by six I-153s of 13 OIAE. After downing four R-5s in the ensuing combat, Gladiators GL-254 and GL-258 were shot down and the third damaged in a forced landing caused by hits.

LLv 28 took over the defence of the southwestern ports and LLv 24 units flew to forward landing grounds close to the Karelian Isthmus, while 25 IAP claimed three Fokker D.XXIs shot down, 68 IAP five Bulldogs in two clashes, and 149 IAP three monoplanes and one biplane fighter.

Six I-16s of 68 IAP lead by StLt Plotnikov engaged in combat with eight Bulldogs, while patrolling in the region of the village of Mäkelä. The task of this group was to cover SB bombers attacking a target in the same area. Soon after the SBs dropped bombs, the I-16s saw the first Bulldog, which flew to the north at an altitude of 2,500m. It was attacked and downed by StLt Plotnikov. According to the pilot's report, the aircraft smoked and fell into the forest.

Just after that, at 1705hrs Russian time, the I-16s turned to the opposite direction and saw a group of R-Z aircraft, which were flying below them, and also seven other Bulldogs. Two

Gladiator pilots of 2/LLv 26 at Ruokolahti in February 1940. Front row from left: 2Lt K. Nevakari, two Danish volunteers, WO L. Lautamäki and Cpl S. Suikkanen. Back row from left: flight leader 1Lt E. Kivinen, Cpl I. Joensuu, MSgt J. Tolkki and 2Lt A. Alitalo. On the last day of February, LLv 26 lost five Gladiators and LLv 24 one Fokker in an air strike on Ruokolahti.

Bulldogs attacked one R-Z and it came over Soviet territory, losing altitude. Lt Safronenko's flight attacked one of these Bulldogs and shot it down. The Bulldog crashed into the forest on the Finnish side.

At the same time, Plotnikov's flight flew towards five other Bulldogs, flying 1,000–1,500m higher and not seeing the Soviet fighters. While climbing, the I-16s got onto the tail of the enemy formation and, all together, fired a burst that missed. The Bulldogs began to turn towards the Soviet fighters. The I-16s continued to turn and shot down one more enemy fighter, which was observed by a command post of a Soviet Army Corps.

Then the flight separated and, in the following combat, Lt Emirov shot down one Bulldog. Emirov was wounded in the hand, while his I-16 received 85 holes, but he returned safely to the airfield. At the same time, Lt Mayev got into a head-on attack with a Bulldog, but simultaneously two other Bulldogs got behind his tail. Mayev's I-16 got 56 bullet holes, but the Bulldog attacked by him was hit and fell to the ground out of control. Mayev got back safely.

For all flying units, 26 February was a day of full activity. LeR 1 continued flying daylight reconnaissance with Gladiators, and at night the Fokker C.Xs both scouted and performed harassment bombings. The campfires had proved to be good target markers and the visibility against the white snowy ground was good.

Soviet bombers attacked Immola, the main base of LLv 24, with large forces. The Fokkers took off for 47 interception missions, trying to engage formations as large as 60 aircraft. However, the Soviet escort fighters made it impossible to engage the bombers. Sgt Tauno Kaarma of LLv 24 escaped injuries when I-153 fighters shot his Fokker FR-85 into flames on the ground at Immola.

Urgently needed on the front, LLv 26 had only ten days of training on their Fiats before their baptism of fire. 1Lt Olli Puhakka took his pair to duel with bombers and fighters south of Kouvola. He shot down one I-16 of 49 IAP and his wingman 2Lt Kauko Linnamaa sent down one DB-3 bomber of 1 AP, KBF (Baltic fleet). Puhakka's first Fiat combat report stated:

At 1440–1520hrs. I chased DB-3 bombers having bombed Kouvola. North of Kouvola I observed below me three I-16s attacking a lone Gladiator. When I dived on the scene I saw only two I-16s, which I attacked, pulling up after every dive. I managed to score hits in both, especially one received long bursts from behind and above behind. After one pull up I saw it exit in a glide. Also the other disappeared from my sight as I had to pay attention to the enemy planes above me.

After that I chased two I-15s, firing at one several bursts straight from behind. Finally it appeared that its engine was not running properly. It flew straight in a shallow dive towards the sea while the other tried to protect it. I left it at the coast between Kotka and Pyhtää, when 15 fighters approached from Suursaari direction.

In combat against the I-16 fighters participated another Fiat, flown by 1Lt Nieminen. The Gladiator was probably piloted by Cpl Paunu.

My plane FA-4 had a few bullet holes, the oxygen bottle punctured among other things. Especially a Fiat with enclosed canopy is easy to take by surprise, since the visibility to the sides and rear is extremely poor.

LLv 44 lost BL-119 on a reconnaissance mission north of Lake Ladoga, being shot down by I-16 fighters of 49 IAP. After a forced landing within Finnish lines, the aircrew survived.

Since 17 February, an order had been given to LeR 4 to bomb Lotinanpelto air base, but the weather did not permit this until 26 February. LLv 46 was declared operational and at 0300hrs took off with eight bombers led by Capt. Kalle Kepsu to attack Lotinanpelto. He reported:

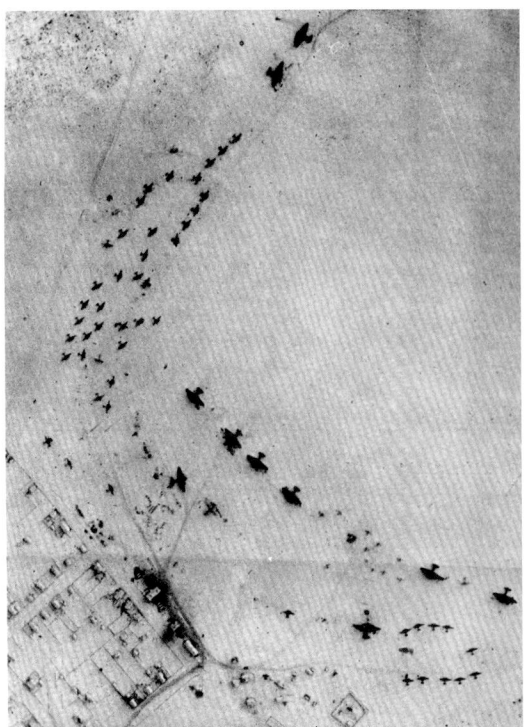

> The squadron carried out an air attack with eight aircraft (BL-130, 128, 124, 129, 133, 132, 126 and 131) in order to bomb aircraft parked at Lotinanpelto airfield. Due to poor visibility en route over Lake Ladoga, the aircraft were separated and the following bombings were recorded: two aircraft bombed the actual target, two aircraft bombed the reserve target, warehouses at Lotinanpelto station, one bombed the railway at Lotinanpelto, two bombed the second reserve target of Vitele and one bombed the artillery batter at Yhinmäki.
>
> As a result, several fires were observed, both at Lotinanpelto and Vitele. Several aircraft were assuming being damaged. Anti-aircraft fire only from Vitele. One fighter was seen. Bombing altitude 300 metres. The enemy thought we were their own and lit the landing lights.

In the afternoon, another three Blenheims of LLv 46 bombed Lotinanpelto again and reported eight aircraft destroyed and the hangar on fire.

At the beginning of the war, LLv 42 had existed only on paper. On 16 January 1940, it was established; Capt. Armas Eskola was put in command and personnel began arriving at the base at Juva. On this day, English crews flew 12 short-nose Blenheims to Juva as new equipment. Meanwhile, two Ripons of LLv 36 were sent out to bomb the installations at Suursaari, but above the target the anti-aircraft guns shot down RI-130, killing both of the aircrew.

On the Soviet side, 25 IAP claimed two and 68 IAP another three Fokker D.XXIs shot down. 49 IAP claimed one Blenheim, north of Lake Ladoga. 10 ABr, KBF claimed four Spitfires[2] (Moranes) shot down in Turku area. At 1450–1600hrs Russian time, five I-16s of 68 IAP carried out a reconnaissance of railroad traffic in the region of Imatra station. During the flight they found and strafed a train, then 7km north of Imatra they discovered an airfield and, at 1535hrs, strafed the aircraft, which were parked under some kind of tents. Four Fokker D.XXIs caught fire and four others did not. At nearby Ruokolahti church, eight Bulldogs took off and attempted to intercept the I-16s. Due to shortage of fuel and ammunition the Soviet fighters avoided combat and fled, the Bulldogs chasing them to Antrea.

On 27 February, LLv 12 observed a huge concentration of Soviet troops in Rokkala-Sommee area and within two days both Lihaniemi and Uuras were full of troops. LLv 24 flew 47 interception sorties southeast of Viipuri, but again the escort fighters did not allow the Fokkers to engage the bombers. LLv 26 lost Fiat FA-12 and 2Lt Eero Malmivuo, who were shot down by I-153 fighters.

All LeR 4 sorties were flown to the Karelian Isthmus. The second attack by the Russians had broken the outer defence lines and the troops approached Viipuri. Over a period of five days, the Blenheims bombed troops, vehicles, railyards and equipment south and southeast

On 26 February 1940, LLv 46 carried out its first mission with the new long-nose Blenheims, attacking Lotinanpelto air base by River Svir with eight bombers. This aerial photograph of Lotinanpelto was taken on 2 February 1940, the situation being quite the same three weeks later. The Russians did not care if the aircraft were in neat lines, open to a successful air raid. There are 11 heavy bombers, at least 50 medium bombers and ten fighters.

2   The Soviets typically misidentified the Moranes as Spitfires.

English pilots flew 12 short-nose Blenheims to Finland on 26 February 1940. Here is BL-134 with covered national insignias and civil registration OH-IPA. Sweden had a ban on military aircraft over its airspace. It was photographed on the ice at Juva on arrival, and the bomber was assigned to 3/LLv 42. (Finnish Air Force)

of Viipuri across 33 sorties. 7 IAP claimed one Finnish fighter shot down, 25 IAP claimed one, and 68 IAP two Fokker D.XXIs destroyed.

Foggy weather prevented all missions on 28 February. On the ground, a Swedish voluntary unit took the front responsibility at Salla in Lapland, while Finnish troops began to transfer to the Karelian Isthmus. On this same day, LLv 16 received five Fokker C.Vs from LLv 14 and transferred them to the north to fly for the Lapland Group.

The last day of the month, 29 February, was the saddest day for the Finnish fighter arm, when Soviet fighters carried out a series of air raids on LLv 24 and 26 bases. Three weeks earlier, Detachment Luukkanen of LLv 24 had moved to Ruokolahti and two Gladiator flights of LLv 26 were there put under his command.

In the morning, 68 IAP fighters shot down one Gladiator, GL-269, killing Cpl Pentti Kosola. At noon a bomber formation was announced to approach Ruokolahti, but it turned out to be the 68 IAP with six Chaikas and 18 Ratas, which took the Gladiators by complete surprise at take-off.

GL-259 (1Lt Carl Kristensen killed), GL-262 (1Lt Aimo Halme killed) and GL-268 (MSgt Olavi Lilja wounded) were immediately destroyed during take-off. In a low-level combat, a further two, GL-261 (1Lt Povl Christensen wounded) and GL-263 (MSgt Jussi Tolkki wounded) were shot down, as was finally Fokker FR-94, piloted by 1Lt Tatu Huhanantti, killing him. Only one I-16 was shot down and another hit the trees while manoeuvring at low altitude.

Kouvola road and railway junction were attacked by 132 aircraft during the course of the day. The Fiats of LLv 26 were given the task of preventing the bombardments. They engaged a nine-plane SB formation of 57 AP, KBF heading towards the town and shot down

Another Blenheim arriving to Juva on 26 February 1940 was OH-IPD. It had the Finnish serial BL-137 and was given to 1/LLv 42. This squadron trained for only one week before being compelled to enter the action, in order to repel the Soviet invasion across the frozen east tip of the Gulf of Finland. The planes wear typical late-1930s British bomber camouflage with black undersides. (Finnish Air Force)

three. 7 IAP claimed eight fighters destroyed on the ground at Utti. 10 ABr, KBF claimed two Spitfires (Moranes) shot down in Turku area. Seventeen I-16s and six I-153s of 68 IAP participated in the raid on Ruokolahti air base. The Soviet pilots claimed ten Bulldogs and eight Fokker D.XXIs. The victories were claimed as follows.

Soviet claims at Ruokolahti

1. Maj. Gil shot down one D.XXI in a head-on attack. The enemy aircraft caught fire, overturned and came down. Gil's second victory was a Bulldog, which got on the tail of Lt Polushkin. This Bulldog also caught fire and went to the ground.
2. StLt Plotnikov attacked a Bulldog, which got on Maj. Gil's tail. The Bulldog began to smoke, came out of control and crashed to the ground.
3. StLt Ivanov attacked and shot down one Bulldog, which got onto Plotnikov's tail. The Bulldog smoked heavily and went to the ground.
4. Lt Sorokin and Lt Nikitin attacked a Fokker, which caught fire and fell out of control from an altitude of 3,200m.
5. StLt Yefimov, Lt Shishov, Lt Terpugov, Lt Orlov and Lt Sapozhnikov downed in a group one Bulldog, which caught fire and crashed to the ground from 70–100m.
6. Lt Polushkin and MlLt. Mazurenko saw a Fokker which attempted to attack their flight. With a swift turn, they got on to the enemy's tail and shot it down with attack from two sides. Enemy caught fire and came to the ground.
7. Lt Shishov saw one Bulldog flying at 100m, attacked it at high speed, overtook it, then turned back and attacked it again. The Bulldog began to smoke and crashed to the ground.
8. MlLt Mazurenko saw that one Fokker got behind his tail. With heavy sideslip. he turned his aircraft 45–50 degrees and the Fokker overtook him. Mazurenko turned back and with a long burst downed the enemy. The Fokker caught fire and crashed to the ground. Mazurenko's aircraft had 36 bullet holes.
9. Lt Orlov dived on the tail of a Bulldog that flew just above the ground and his fire forced it to crash to the ground.
10. Lt Platonov pursued one Bulldog. Attacking from behind he forced it to dive. Platonov followed it and continued to fire. The Bulldog got into a spin and crashed to the ground.
11. Lt Popov after the attack of the airfield was climbing altitude, when he saw I-16 and I-153, chasing a Bulldog. The Bulldog with split-S evaded their attack. That time Popov attacked the enemy and when the Bulldog was recovering from the dive Popov fired it and set it on fire.
12. Lt Mayev while climbing to altitude saw a Fokker, which got behind an I-16 and began to fire. Mayev attacked the Fokker from behind and set it on fire. The Fokker came out of control to the ground.
13. MlLt Soldatov dropped bombs on the enemy aircraft parked on the frozen lake. After that he was attacked by two Fokkers, but using the manoeuvrability and climbing performance of his I-153, he evaded the attack and climbed to the Soviet group. He saw that one Fokker was pursuing an I-16 and decided to attack it. The enemy decided to outturn him, but Soldatov manoeuvred behind it and fired several long bursts. The enemy aircraft went into a dive. Soldatov followed it and observed that the Fokker crashed into the forest.
14. Lt Konyukhov shot down one Fokker in a head-on attack. For some reason, the enemy aircraft did not fire in return. The Fokker began to smoke and hit the ground out of control.
15. Lt Nikitin attacked a Bulldog twice, and shot it down. It fell into the forest and caught fire.

16. Lt Fyodorov having approached to the target saw one Bulldog at 2,200m. Fyodorov got behind it and shot it down with two bursts. The Bulldog dived vertically and fell north of Salvisaari island. After that, Fyodorov dropped the bombs on one Fokker, which was taxiing on the lake. Just after taking off, this Fokker caught fire and hit the ice.

March 1940

When the Soviet advance across the Karelian Isthmus seemed to be halted at the last defensive line of the Finns, just southeast of Viipuri, the Red armies decided to attack the rear of the defences by crossing the frozen Viipurinlahti (Gulf of Vyborg). In other parts of the front, the Soviet advance had earlier come to an end. North of Lake Ladoga, the Russians fiercely held the encirclements, while facing a slow starvation. The Soviets attempted to advance to the rear of the Finns, in order to help to break the encirclements, but these efforts ultimately failed.

On 1 March, the Soviet assault towards the city of Viipuri was repelled. In the rear of the Karelian Isthmus front the fighter bases were under continuous air raids, both from fighters and light bombers. The flights of LLv 24 continued to use several forward-landing grounds, frozen lakes, in order to stay operational. During February, LLv 24 had claimed 27 aircraft destroyed, but its serviceability at the end of the month was down to just 22 Fokkers. LLv 26 delivered the remaining Gladiators to LeR 1 squadrons LLv 12 and 14 and became fully equipped with Fiat G.50 fighters.

13 IAP and 12 OIAE, both of KBF, attacked Utti air base and claimed seven Fokkers and four Bulldogs destroyed. This was a remarkable achievement considering that the base was now completely empty of Finnish aircraft.

On 2 March there was plenty of activity all over Finland. LeR 1 flew the regular reconnaissance and harassment bombardment missions on the Karelian Isthmus. LLv 24 was resting and overhauling its fighters at Lemi after extensive and exhaustive fighting. LLv 28 shot down two bombers in southwestern Finland and chased one fighter to Estonia, shooting it down. The Moranes of the 2nd Flight entered into two encounters. The pair of 2Lt Pauli Massinen destroyed one DB-3 bomber of 1 AP, KBF out of a large formation west of Turku. Massinen wrote in his combat report:

Gladiator GL-256 of 2/LLv 12 in field servicing at Konnunsuo forward base, on 2 March 1940. The Gladiators allowed the unit to perform daylight reconnaissance missions in spite of the enemy's fighter presence over the Karelian Isthmus. The period's standard British black and white wings have a mismatch. (Finnish Air Force)

At 1325hrs. The enemy formation had arrived by surprise. I was south of the city waiting for the formation to return. I flew 1,000m higher that the enemy escadrille returning southwards. I approached from the side and above, diving from behind. By additional speed I caught the formation easily. I attacked the last plane, which was a little separated from the others. I fired a short burst to the fuselage from slightly behind and below, when the gunner ceased firing. Thereafter I fired at the right engine making a few short dives. It started to leak fuel and finally caught fire.

Now an enemy fighter was diving towards me and I considered it best to break off the duel by a dive, especially when only the centre gun had ammunition left. According to air surveillance the bomber had exploded mid-air and the remnants fallen to the archipelago. The bomber was a DB-3.

As my personal opinion I dare to state that the Morane is a good fighter when it comes to speed and manoeuvrability, but the armament is weak. The optical sight is malfunctioning too often, the machine-guns lose their aim and the ammunition count is too small. The bullets did not penetrate the enemy armour either. My plane was MS-318.

In the afternoon, future 42-victory ace and Mannerheim Cross winner, Cpl Urho Lehtovaara of 2/LLv 28 claimed one SB bomber out of a nine-plane formation destroyed. He reported:

I scrambled at 1430hrs towards Loimaa, to where a bomber formation was approaching from the south. When arriving above Loimaa I observed a formation of nine bombers, which flew in a tight echelon northwards, changing the course immediately to south. I approached the formation from the rear climbing behind thin clouds above it.

I targeted my first attack to the plane on the right wing closing-in in a 45-degree dive, the enemy gunner opened fire as soon as I went in the dive. I approached my target to 150m straight behind and gave a short burst, when the gunner disappeared and the gun remained pointing up. During this time the left wing – 5 planes – of the formation had slowed down straight to my side and opened fire, when I had to pull up and break off the fight.

I repeated my attack instantly to the last plane on the left wing, which was flying about 100m behind the others. I approached in a steep dive from the right and behind, when the gunner and the port engine came to the same aiming line. I fired a short burst, when I observed that the left engine produced a stream of smoke, banked to the left down and disappeared from my sight.

After first pulling up I dived after the falling bomber, to make sure that it would be shot down. But due to big difference in altitude I did neither catch the bomber nor did I see it fall down to the ground. During the dive I had lost so much altitude that I would not have caught the other bombers before the Estonian coast, so I gave up the chase and returned to the base. My plane was MS-326.

On this day, 38 IAP claimed two Fokker D.XXIs shot down and 7 DBAP, KBF one more in central Finland, while 8 and 10 ABr, KBF claimed having destroyed six Brewsters in the Turku area.

On 3 March, the Russians commenced their advance across the frozen Viipurinlahti. At 1400hrs, the Gladiator pilots of LLv 12 gave alarming reports that the first units were near the coast at Vilajoki, in the rear of the main defence line. In the darkness, LLv 12 bombed the troops at Johannes. LLv 14 was on the eastern part of the Karelian Isthmus and attacked the Russian troops trying to cross River Vuoksi at Vuosalmi.

The Soviet troops had managed to cross Viipurinlahti over the ice on 4 March, forming a bridgehead at Vilaniemi and Häränpääniemi. Troops and columns kept flowing across the ice from Pulliniemi and Tuppura. All Finnish regiments were thrown in to repel this serious threat. LeR 4 was ordered to attack with all available forces against the enemy, which was intruding to the west coast of Viipurinlahti. This was a baptism of fire for both LLv 44 and 42, which flew strike sorties with five aircraft to Kiuskeri and Iso-Kalastaja in the outer Gulf of Finland, where enemy troops were marching towards the Finnish coast.

On 5 March LLv 12 flew a regular reconnaissance mission to Viipurinlahti, reporting the following:

At 0600–0700hrs. Altitude 1,000–100m. Planes GL-277 Capt. Maunula and GL-275 2Lt Marttila. Observations:

Between Pikku-Kalastaja and Satamaniemi 19 men in snow suit. At the edges of Vilalahti bay random tanks, 5 on the east coast and 10–12 in the north bend.

From Teikarsaari to Pitkäniemi thin columns of infantry, the head 500m from Teikarsaari. Between Melasaari and Teikarsaari infantry and horse vehicle column. From the north tip of Teikarsaari straight to north 4 trucks and 30 men.

On the winter road between Teikarsaari and Tuppura solitary trucks. On the winter road from Teikarsaari to Pulliniemi four armoured cars. On the north coast at Pulliniemi 20–30 tanks spread around. At Vatnuori village campfires and 20 tanks.

On the winter road from Kaaliala to Revonsaari 1km long column of infantry and trucks, ending in three armoured cars, heading to Pulliniemi. On the west coast of Revonsaari at Repola village an eight km long truck column, heading north.

In the middle of the road between Revonsaari and Makslahti light traffic, possibly a command post. Nothing observed at Uuraansaari. Fires at Revonsaari. Targets strafed by machine-gun fire.

LLv 14 was moved to Viipurinlahti from the eastern part of the Karelian Isthmus to repel the invasion. The morning mission report said:

Aircraft and crews: FK-110 2Lt Ala-Panula and 1Lt Honkanen, FK-107 2Lt Arkko and MSgt Harju, GL-267 1Lt Ollikainen, GL-273 1Lt Pitkänen, GL-274 1Lt Kuula, GL-276 2Lt Malinen, GL-278 SSgt Perälä and GL-279 Cpl Roine. Task: Reconnaissance, bombing and strafing on the columns and camps in Häränpäänniemi-Pulliniemi-Teikarsaari-Vilaniemi. Take-off at 0605hrs and return at 0730hrs. Observations:

On ice between Pulliniemi and Teikarsaari a continuous row of trucks towards Tuppuransaari island. Tuppuransaari-Vilaniemi ice road full of troops, trucks and tanks. At Vilaniemi on the beach 20 tanks. Flak battery at Teikarsaari shooting at us. At Teikarsaari one kilometre long column of troops heading SE from Teikarsaari. At Vilaniemi bay several company strong waves of troops heading towards the beach. Dropped 2x50kg, 3x25kg and 6x3,5kg bombs and strafed with 2,000 rounds. Enemy fighters at 5 kilometres distance north of Viipuri.

In the afternoon, 2/LLv 14 got an order to shoot down an artillery spotting plane between Äyräpää and Pölläkkälä. 1Lt Tauno Ollikainen took off with six Gladiators at 1325hrs for a 55-minute mission, as told by the mission report:

Planes and crews: GL-267 1Lt Ollikainen, GL-273 1Lt Pitkänen, GL-274 1Lt Kuula, GL-276 2Lt Malinen, GL-278 SSgt Perälä and GL-279 Cpl Roine. At 1400hrs the artillery fire control plane was not met.

Between Kihlasaari and Kuussaari two I-153s attacked SSgt Perälä's plane. In the ensuing curve battle SSgt Perälä shot one of these down with a short burst. The altitude was then about 150 metres. 7,7 mm ammunition spent 200 rounds.

The Chaika was also later confirmed as lost, belonging to 68 IAP.

With Soviet troops vulnerable on the ice, Viipurinlahti also drew the attention of Soviet fighters. Capt. Eino Luukkanen of LLv 24 led several strafing missions and describes one encounter with the defending fighters in the early evening as follows:

I am breaking the radio silence and order the formation (15 Fokkers) out of the clouds. Now we are playing the enemy by approaching from their direction in the south. I bank to the left and lead the formation into a dive. There seems to be no lack of the targets, because the 4 kilometres distance between Tuppura and Vilaniemi is full of columns, cars, trucks and tanks. Above Uuras circles an I-16 squadron and another fighter unit is on the other side of the gulf over Ristiniemi. I continue the shallow dive; the sooner we hit the better for us. The range to the nearest targets is one kilometre, when the air around us fills with explosions and tracers of anti-aircraft fire. Both white and black explosion clouds puff close to us, which attracts the enemy fighters after us.

My first burst hits an infantry column, next in the sight is a line of trucks and finally I manage to fire at two tanks. The bullets of our rifle-calibre machine guns do not seem to have any effect on the latter, at least the tracers bounced away from the armour plates. After my strafing run I look back and ascertain that the rest of the formation follows my recent example.

Immediately after the attack the return begins – first at low level to the west and then banking to the north towards our base, so that the enemy would not discover our location in case someone was tailing us.

The top cover was engaged in a fighter duel with 25 IAP as told by Sgt Eero Kinnunen:

At 1730hrs. I flew as the wingman of the top cover pair of the 1st flight. Our mission was to shoot enemy columns on the ice between Tuppuransaari and Vilaniemi. When our flight dived towards the columns, I saw during the dive three I-16s, one of which tried to get behind the tail of one Fokker. I shot at it from left and above, when it pulled away towards Teikarsaari.

But then I observed tracers in Vilaniemi direction. I flew there and saw one Fokker flying at the deck to south-west with one I-16 just 50m behind it and shooting. When I got within 150 metres I shot at it from right and behind. It then pulled up twisting a little to the left. During the pull-up I could fire at it as long as the Fokker could follow.

After this I continued back to the base. The mentioned I-16 did not even try to follow me. The other Fokker under fire was flown by 2Lt Savonen. The enemy planes which I saw were not flying in any formation. The wreck was found north of Vilaniemi. My plane was FR-109.

All LeR 4 squadrons flew to Viipurinlahti on 33 sorties. The first ones were made in small groups and thereafter in single planes, as soon as the Blenheims had rearmed and refuelled at their bases. Maj. Armas Eskola commanding LLv 42 led one of these missions and he reported:

Luukkanen: Strafing Viipurinlahti, 5 March 1940

The final Soviet offensive in the Winter War came across the ice of Viipurinlahti (Gulf of Vyborg) to the rear of the main defence line. The attack began on 3 March and, within two days, the Red Army managed to get two bridgeheads – one at Vilaniemi and another at Häränpäänniemi. Against this very serious threat, the whole Finnish Air Force was cast in, assisted effectively by the coastal artillery.

Across six days, the Finns were able to sweep the ice clean, causing huge losses to the enemy. All three fighter squadrons flew strafing missions, while bombers of LeR 1 and LeR 4 first bombed in groups and then by single planes after rearming and refuelling. 3/LLv 24 leader Capt. Eino Luukkanen headed several strafing missions, with up to 15 Fokkers punishing the enemy troops and vehicles on the ice, which were completely without shelter. In spite of the tens of fighters patrolling over Viipurinlahti, all units performed their missions regardless of losses, which remained quite light, both parties losing four aircraft.

LLv 42 bombed with five aircraft (BL-145, 143, 142, 140 and 137). The aircraft were separated in the fighter interception and the attacks were conducted individually. At 1605hrs two aircraft (each 4x 100kg and 4x 120lbs bombs) bombed troops and vehicles on the coast of Melansaari island, one aircraft (1x 100kg, others did not fall) troops at Teikarsaari island and one troops at Tuppura island. One aircraft (4x 100kg) misjudged the target and bombed Ristniemi.

On the east coast of Teikarsaari island 20–30 tanks, heading to Melansaari Island. At Melansaari plenty of troops. On the coast jam among the vehicles. In the woods plenty of troops. From Tuppura island to Teikarsaari island 500 metres long column with horse-drawn vehicles. Anti-aircraft fire from Melansaari island.

North of Melansaari three I-16s attacked. They got inside the firing range, but no effects. On return one I-16 attacked at Virolahti, but did not get into a firing position.

On ten occasions, 7 IAP claimed ten fighters, three bombers and two reconnaissance aircraft. 54 IAB, KBF claimed a further three Bulldogs. 42 DBAP claimed one fighter shot down.

According to 68 IAP war diary, the Soviet pilots Povoroznikov and Semin saw a flight of four Bulldogs, while escorting a group of SB bombers. Two Bulldogs escaped into the clouds, while the other two engaged in combat. At 1540hrs, Povoroznikov shot down one Bulldog in the region of Vuoksenranta. Semin got onto the tail of the other enemy aircraft and while making a tight turn at the altitude of 150–200m, got into a spin and crashed.

The battles at the coast at Vilaniemi were fierce on 6 March 1940, and both sides suffered heavy casualties. The Finns threw in the last reserves and managed to prevent the Soviets expanding the invasion area. Alone here, 70 Soviet tanks were destroyed. LLv 24 flew 18 strafing sorties against the troops, columns and vehicles on the ice of Viipurinlahti, while LeR 4 bombers carried out 16 sorties to Viipurinlahti. 7 IAP claimed a further three bombers shot down.

Fiat FA-10 of 3/LLv 26 at the edge of Haukkajärvi lake, near Utti, in March 1940. The refuelling is about to start from a hand pump from a 200l barrel, which was towed on a sledge. Only one flight of Fiats saw combat and they claimed 11 air victories during the last fortnight of the Winter War.

On 7 March, LLv 14 flew escort for Finnish troop transfers west of Viipuri and six Gladiators were involved in a combat with three I-153s of 148 IAP, two of which were shot down at the cost of two damaged Gladiators. The mission report stated as follows:

Aircraft and crews: GL-267 1Lt Ollikainen, GL-273 1Lt Pitkänen, GL-274 1Lt Kuula, GL-276 2Lt Malinen, GL-278 SSgt Perälä and GL-279 Cpl Roine. Mission between 1435 and 1610hrs.

When patrolling over Tienhaara two pairs of I-16s were observed, no contact. Over Tervajoki village met three I-153s, which pulled over, turned and attacked the second pair. The first pair turned around and started the combat, which was carried out between 1515 and 1525hrs, from 300m to the surface. The wind shifted the participants west of Tervajoki.

Two I-153s were shot down and they both crashed in the forest. 1Lt Ollikainen claimed one witnessed by 1Lt Kuula. The other was claimed by 2Lt Malinen and witnessed by 1Lt Pitkänen. Cpl Roine made a successful emergency landing to Löytöjärvi after being hit in the fuel tank. SSgt Perälä´s wing touched the wing on an I-153 breaking the starboard tip of the upper wing.

On this day, LLv 24 flew 43 strafing sorties to Viipurinlahti. The tasks had become very difficult and dangerous. The Soviets had placed anti-aircraft artillery units on both sides of the gulf in addition to continuous combat air patrols by large fighter formations, often the whole regiment of 50 aircraft.

The situation had become critical and two flights of Moranes of LLv 28 were transferred closer to the front on the Karelian Isthmus. They immediately joined the strafing attacks over Viipurinlahti.

LeR 4 attacked the target on the ice of Viipurinlahti invaders on the shore on 24 sorties. Two Blenheims, BL-144 of LLv 42 and BL-122 of LLv 46, were shot down, wounding one and killing five airmen. Across eight encounters, 7 IAP claimed seven bombers and one fighter. Meanwhile, 25 IAP claimed one Blenheim and 148 IAP three aircraft more.

On 8 March, peace negotiations commenced in Moscow. The Soviets had advanced to Viipuri-Helsinki main road in the invasion area. LeR 4 kept hammering the Soviet troops at

Fokker FR-110 'blue/white 7' of 3/LLv 24 lost the port ski in flight, and 2Lt Olli Mustonen made a skilful forced landing to Joroinen on 8 April 1940. This machine was assigned to WO Viktor Pyötsiä, who in this plane scored seven and a half air victories, which were marked on the fin as white bars.

Viipurinlahti on 14 bombing missions, while LLv 24 flew 19 strafing missions. The supply of ammunition, equipment and fuel to the invasion spearhead was made severely more difficult. 7 IAP claimed a further three bombers shot down.

On 9 March the Soviet troops pressed on closer to the city of Viipuri. However, the fronts bent but did not break. LeR 1 kept close watch of the enemy ground movements while LeR 2 and LeR 4 kept on strafing and bombing the troops in the invasion area, and attacking the supply columns. LLv 26 claimed one fighter shot down over Viipurinlahti. LLv 28 lost Morane MS-322 to flak, wounding 1Lt Erkki Lupari. On the other hand, it claimed two fighters, with 2Lt Jouko Myllymäki relating of the latter:

At 1110–1300hrs. When participating on a strafing mission to Viipurinlahti and returning to the base I observed three I-16 fighters behind me. I instantly took a dive via a half-roll and after an aileron turn took the previous course flying at the deck. Now they were inside the shooting range and started firing. I took evasive action by banking. These three fighters stayed all the time pretty well tightly together. During the curving I did not pay enough attention to the terrain and when flying down at the deck I became disoriented. After a while I recognized having arrived to the west coast of the Karelian Isthmus.

Now I got two three-plane I-16 patrols more after me. These patrols flew in a line, wing trios 50m higher. When I began curving to left and right, the patrol on the curve side pushed down and started firing. I started looking for a higher hill, around which I could turn and escape to the north, as I was already over the Karelian Isthmus.

When I arrived at a frozen lake, which had an enemy base, one I-16 took off towards me. I shot the remaining 20–30 rounds into it aiming at the pilot. The plane pulled up and while banking in the shelter of the lake shore I saw it crash on the ice.

I now got the course to the north and pulled up into the clouds. They were so thin that the enemy planes followed me. When I went down to the deck I managed to increase the distance, when seven enemy planes gave up the chase, both wing patrols and one plane from the centre patrol. I broke off quite easily from these two enemies by my slightly greater speed as I did not need to perform any greater evasive turns. I came back to Viipurinlahti,

Morane MS318 'yellow 3' of 2/LLv 28 at Säkylä in early March 1940. It shows one of two known victory markings, a silver star on the rudder. It denoted the downing of a DB-3 bomber on 2 March, by 2Lt Pauli Massinen. In front of the fighter are French mechanics, Decousser and Levard. The fuselage insignia still needs a clean-up.

Blenheim BL-129 of 3/LLv 46 being refuelled by hand pump between missions at Luonetjärvi on 7 March 1940. The plane was assigned to the flight leader, 1Lt Olavi Siirilä. Both inter-wing tanks took 630l and both outer-wing tanks 425l fuel, which for the Mercury XV engines of Blenheim IV was100 octane. (SA-kuva)

where these two enemies gave up the chase because the distance had grown enough that there was no point in continuing. I returned to my base at Utti. My plane was MS-330.

7 IAP claimed during seven occasions eight fighters and one bomber shot down.

On 10 March, LLv 10 was transferred to Puumala during the course of the day. LLv 14 lost Gladiator GL-279 to I-153 fighters, killing the flight leader 1Lt Tauno Ollikainen. The numerous Soviet fighters that were patrolling over Viipurinlahti, combined with occasional snowfall, did not permit the fighters of LeR 2 to press home strafing attacks. The bombers of LeR 4 carried out 24 sorties to the gulf area. LLv 46 lost BL-133 to the fighters, killing the three-man aircrew.

In Lapland, six large TB-3 bombers appeared over Rovaniemi. A pair of Gladiators from F 19 was sent into the air to meet them and, after a chase, shot down one attacker at Kemijärvi. 7 IAP claimed one bomber and one fighter, and 68 IAP one Bulldog.

Seven days after the attack started, the ice over Viipurinlahti had been swept clean, with heavy casualties for the Russians. The Soviet advance on land had also been stopped, and the city of Viipuri remained unconquered. On 11 March, LeR 1 employed LLv 10 and 12 to the Viipurinlahti. The reconnaissance of the latter provided a good picture of the spearheads of the Soviet advance. The bombings were more of a harassment nature due to the modest bombload of the Fokker C.X. LLv 14 came to assist in interception and claimed three fighters for the loss of one Gladiator.

The Fokker D.XXIs of LLv 24 flew 154 assault sorties, claimed one I-16 shot down and lost one Fokker in return. LLv 26 carried out ten strafing sorties, while LLv 28 was out on 20 sorties, claiming two fighters while one Morane was shot down by anti-aircraft fire.

LeR 4 had flown 144 sorties to the Viipurinlahti. The Soviets flew continuous combat air patrol over the gulf and I-153 fighters destroyed three Blenheims, one from LLv 42 and two from LLv 46. On the other hand, the rear gunners claimed three fighters sent down.

The last combats were fought over southern Finland, where fighter formations as large as 200 were observed. LLv 24 was involved in the fighter duels with no results.

OPPOSITE FRONT LINE AT THE END OF THE WAR, 13 MARCH 1940

Morane MS305 'white 6' of 3/LLv 28 takes off from Pyhäniemi ice base at Hollola on 13 March 1940, the last day of the Winter War. Except for the armament, the Morane was considered superior to all Soviet fighters. Two flights of Moranes had assisted in repelling the Soviet invasion across the frozen Viipurinlahti a few days earlier. (SA-kuva)

In the defence of Kouvola, the Fiats recorded LLv 26's last air victory in the Winter War, as told by 1Lt Olli Puhakka:

At 1340–1420hrs. Just north of Kouvola I attacked an enemy formation, which consisted of five DB-3 bombers. I followed them south to Elimäki attacking the plane at the right wing. After a long burst the right engine appeared to catch fire, which went soon out. The plane began to leave a dark trail of smoke, remaining in its formation.

I moved then after the plane at the left wing because it had separated a little from the formation. I first shot in the fuselage, which got several hits judging by the flashes of the incendiary bullets. After that I fired to the left engine, which began to pour white smoke.

I ran out of ammunition and banked away. Then flying higher and behind me two I-153s went in a dive to attack me, but I broke away by a dive. At the beginning MSgt Tuominen in my patrol was attacking the same bombers. Cartridges spent 600. My plane was FA-21.

Furthermore, the last combats over southern Finland occurred, where enemy formations as large as 200 were observed. LLv 28 shot down three DB-3s of 7 DBAP, as the last victories in the Winter War. 2Lt Martti Inehmo filed in the combat report:

At 1445hrs I took off for a combat air patrol led by 1Lt Linkola. The start took place at Hollola and we flew to Lahti-Kouvola railway, which the Russians had been bombing along the whole day. We climbed to 3,500m searching from both the north and south side of the rails. When approaching Koria station from the west we observed a large enemy formation (70–80 planes) bombing just this station from an altitude of 2,500m.

The lead plane had obviously not observed the two nine-plane formations following the main part and when attacking became a target of the fierce machine-gun fire sent from the nose turrets of these planes. This firing stopped when I banked into a dive towards them and attacked the left-wing plane. Now the fire from the fuselage turrets was aimed at me.

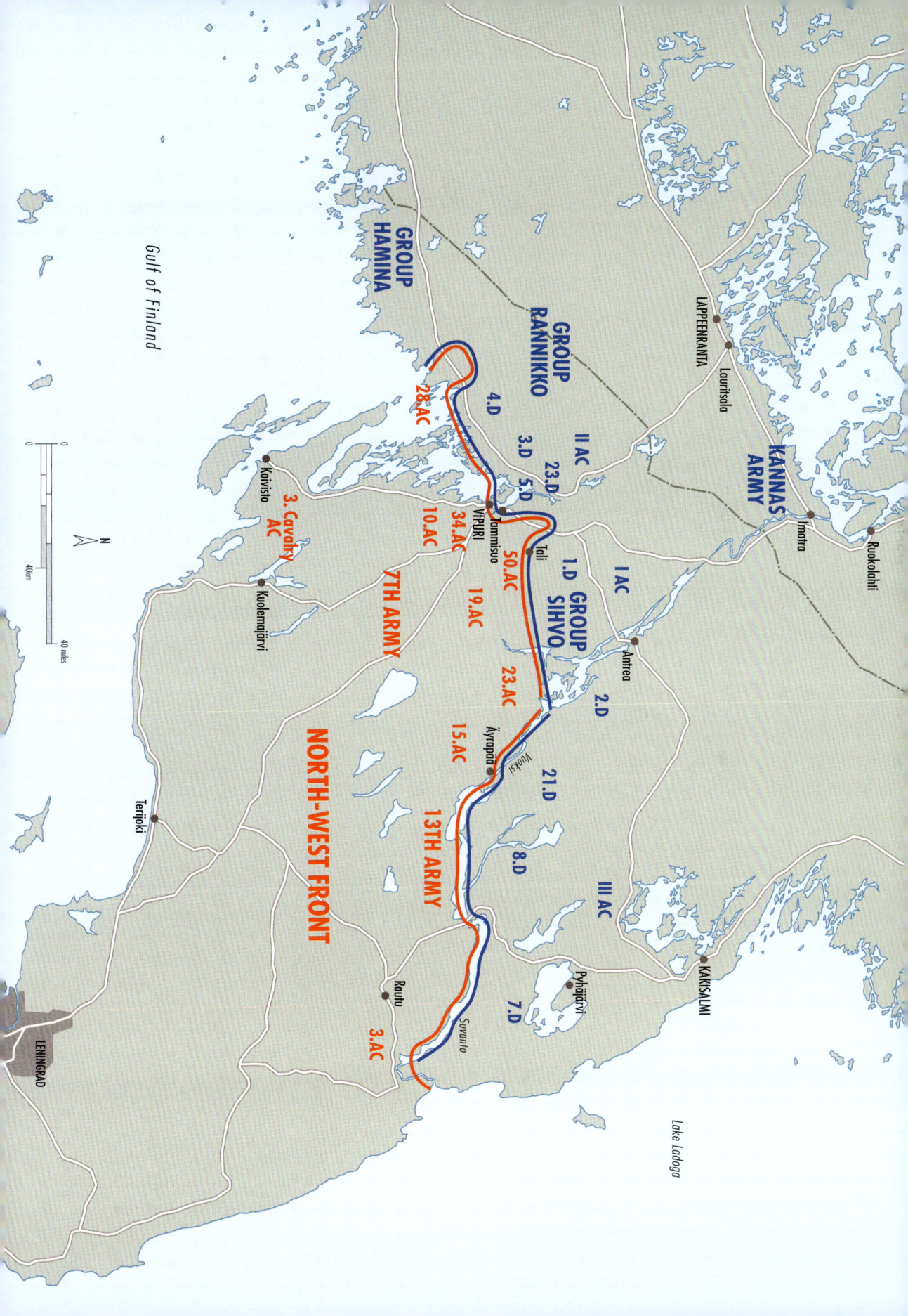

Gulf of Finland

LAPPEENRANTA
Lauritsala

KANNAS ARMY

GROUP HAMINA

GROUP RANNIKKO

Imatra

Ruokolahti

28.AC

4.D

3.D

23.D

II AC

5.D

Koivisto

3. Cavalry AC

34.AC

10.AC

VIPURI

Tammisuo

Tali

50.AC

1.D GROUP SIHVO

I AC

Antrea

2.D

Kuolemajärvi

7TH ARMY

19.AC

23.AC

15.AC

Äyräpää

Vuoksi

21.D

8.D

III AC

NORTH-WEST FRONT

13TH ARMY

Terijoki

Rautu

Pyhäjärvi

7.D

KÄKISALMI

3.AC

Suvanto

LENINGRAD

Lake Ladoga

N

0   40 km
0   40 miles

Blenheim BL-128 of 3/LLv 46 is pushed by manpower out of Luonetjärvi hangar, on 8 March 1940. WO Onni Räikkönen was the regular pilot. During a seven-day period this plane flew ten sorties to Viipurinlahti in repelling the Soviet invasion across the ice. (SA-kuva)

I dived too soon towards the enemy planes leaving very little time to shoot. I had to break off behind the DB-3 bomber, down left to the sunny side. During this attack the next two enemy planes dropped back to the side of my target and fired at me all the time.

I stayed with them at about three kilometres' distance, until they were again in an echelon. Now I attacked again the same enemy plane on the left wing. I managed to fire at close range long bursts to the left engine, when it at first started to pour smoke and then also flames.

Also during this attack the next two planes dropped back on my wing, firing. One burst hit my engine cutting oil lines and I was forced to break off to the side and down. I made a forced landing on the ice of Ruuhijärvi, when my plane MS-304 was damaged more after ending on the nose.

On the Soviet side, 15 IAP claimed one Spitfire (Morane), 7 DBAP another Spitfire (Morane) and one Fokker D.XXI shot down.

On 12 March, snowstorms in southern Finland prevented most of the flying, and the following day, 13 March 1940, the Winter War ended at 1100hrs with the peace negotiated in Moscow.

In addition to the daily Soviet claims, the following claims made by regular Soviet air force bomber units have not been included in the text: five fighters by 5 OSAP in Lapland, 14 fighters by 31 SBAP over the Karelian Isthmus, 35 fighters by 35 SBAP over Finland and 38 fighters by 54 SBAP over Finland. These numbers are not officially confirmed.

ANALYSIS

Finnish Air Force statistics

Lentorykmentti 1 had performed 894 reconnaissance sorties during the war, dropping 66.7 tons of bombs. By squadron, the sorties were divided as follows: LLv 10 flew 135, LLv 12 flew 374, LLv 14 flew 234, and LLv 16 flew 151. Ten aircraft were lost on operations and 17 airmen were killed or missing in action, while two became prisoners of war.

Lentorykmentti 2 fighters had flown 3,486 sorties, claiming 170 aircraft shot down with another 70 damaged. It produced ten aces, and lost 23 fighters in action. By squadron, these sorties were split thus: LLv 24 flew 2,388 sorties (with 122 kills, and ten aircraft and seven pilots lost). LLv 26 flew 1,170 sorties (with 34 kills, and 12 aircraft and seven pilots lost), LLv 28 flew 288 sorties (with 14 kills and one aircraft lost).

Lentorykmentti 4 bomber squadrons had performed 423 sorties, by squadrons: LLv 44 flew 209, LLv 46 flew 152 and LLv 46 flew 62 sorties, with a total of 131 tons of bombs dropped. Seven Blenheims and 13 crew members were lost in action. The rear gunners had shot down five fighters.

LLv 36 had flown 186 sorties, losing two aircraft and four crew members. T-LLv 39 flew 61 sorties with no losses. The Test Flight flew 89 sorties, claiming nine air victories and losing one aircraft and pilot.

The Swedish volunteer unit Flygflottilj 19 flew 464 sorties, claiming eight kills and losing four aircraft, while two crew members were killed and two became prisoners of war.

In all, the Finnish Air Force flew 5,693 sorties, and claimed 207 aircraft destroyed and lost 48 warplanes on operations. The anti-aircraft guns took a toll of a further 314 aircraft. Most wrecks of the claimed aircraft could be found, since they came down on Finnish soil.

Recent research in Russian archives has shown the Soviet losses to be 980 aircraft, over half of which were on operations. This is well in line with the total Finnish claims of 521 warplanes. 897 Soviet airmen were lost, either killed, missing in action, or taken as prisoners of war.

Fokker FR-117 'white 8' of 1/LLv 24 collided in the landing run to a camouflage barn at Joroinen on 8 April 1940. During the Winter War it was flown by 2Lt Olli Puhakka, who was on assignment from LLv 26. He claimed five kills, hence becoming an ace. Puhakka was later awarded the Mannerheim Cross after the Continuation War, having gained 46 air victories.

Pilots, observers and gunners of LLv 44 at Joroinen on 13 March 1940. From left: 2Lt H. Huttunen, MSgt U. Oksala, Sgt E. Pulliainen, 2Lt E. Halme, 2Lt E. Nordgren, Sgt V. Laukas, 1Lt A. Melasniemi, WO T. Parikka, 2Lt E. Pohjanheimo, 1Lt R. Moilanen, 2Lt O. Hyttinen and 1Lt A. Platan. Oksala was an excellent bomber pilot and later became a Mannerheim Cross winner in the Continuation War.

According to the Soviet-era records, the Soviet air forces flew 100,970 sorties on the Finnish front, claiming 427 aerial victories and losing 261 aircraft. The claims have been adjusted in later research (1988) to 388 aircraft: 188 by fighters, 146 by bombers and 54 by the Baltic Fleet air forces. This is still very far from matching the actual Finnish loss figure of 48 warplanes in combat.

Soviet analysis

In the Soviet Union, the analysis and conclusions of the gigantic losses were made in complete secrecy. The people were kept in the dark by the highly-visible publishing of lists of new 'Heroes of the Soviet Union' and other award recipients. The celebration of men returning alive from the front was also kept ongoing.

Among the bomber aircrews, a very obvious shortcoming was poor training. Inadequate navigation skills, in particular, caused considerable losses, both operationally and non-operationally. This had already led to the establishment of a new training facility near Moscow on 29 March 1940.

Early in the Winter War, it was learnt that larger bomber formations were too difficult to lead efficiently, since they could not operate from crowded, snowy and icy airfields. This was a clear reason for the very modest bombardment results. From January 1940 onwards, the bomber units on a mission usually consisted one regiment at most.

On 5 April 1940, the NKVD (the notorious Soviet counter-intelligence agency) compiled a detailed 119-page report of the most serious shortcomings of the frontal aviation units. Among the technical flaws were unreliable M-87 engines (on the DB-3), poor self-defence of the bombers (dead angles), poor fire protection (lack of self-sealing fuel tanks), lack of armour, improperly functioning machine guns, malfunctioning small bomb containers, unintentionally exploding bombs, lack of radios and navigation equipment, and unsuitable ground equipment for winter conditions.

Operative shortcomings were incomplete orders, hasty change of orders, inadequate intelligence and enemy knowledge, lack of maps, firing at friendly planes, bombing friendly troops, and collisions, both in the air and on the ground. Furthermore, Soviet operational intentions were exposed to the enemy by repeating the same flight paths and poor radio discipline (if the plane had a radio).

Fokker FR-116 of 5/Llv 26 at Joroinen in early April 1940, still in pristine condition, a couple of weeks after the end of the Winter War. The fighter was assigned to 2Lt Kauko Linnamaa, who was in command from Llv 26. Barely visible, there is a tactical number 'blue 4' on the rudder.

On 17 April 1940, the central committee of the Bolshevik party arranged a top-secret critical meeting on the Winter War for the top brass, led by Marshal Kliment Voroshilov and attended by dictator Joseph Stalin. All the highest commanders of the Red Army were present, including most armies' air force commanders. The attendees were encouraged to speak freely, but the meeting turned almost into an interrogation. The CO of north-west army air forces, Lt Gen. Yegveniy Ptuhin, and Spanish Civil War ace, Maj. Gen. Pavel Rytshagov, both spoke freely and criticized the leadership including Stalin, but the cost was high, for both were executed later.

Almost all of the criticism concerned the bomber aviation, since the fighter clashes were actually quite rare, especially after the Finnish ban on engaging Soviet fighters in combat. The Soviet fighter pilots had, however, discovered that their basic formation, a trio, was less effective than the Finnish pair. But it took nearly two years before the finger-four was adopted in the Soviet air forces.

Bombing statistics

The Finnish statistics of the Soviet bomber offensive would show 690 attacks against civilian targets in the homeland. These saw 55,000 explosive bombs and 41,000 incendiaries dropped. On 440 occasions, the targets were strafed with machine guns.

In total, 965 civilians were killed, 540 severely wounded and another 1,300 lightly wounded. Some 157 stone buildings were destroyed and another 99 burnt, plus 600 damaged. Meanwhile, 1,800 wooden houses were destroyed and 4,100 damaged. Below are the statistics for some of the 690 locations that were raided repeatedly:

Location	Raids	Enemy aircraft deployed to location	Bombs	Killed
Hanko	72	260	1,100	6
Viipuri	64	1400	4,700	38
Turku	61	440	2,550	52
Kouvola	39	850	1,200	28
Elisenvaara	39	280	1,000	35
Lappeenranta	36	550	1,800	37
Rovaniemi	19	170	700	25
Tampere	12	260	1,000	17
Helsinki	8	70	350	97

Houses collapsed and on fire at downtown Helsinki on 30 November 1939, following the Soviet bombardment of civilian targets in the capital, on the first day of the Winter War. The result was worldwide disapproval, and the Soviet Union's expulsion from the League of Nations. This event gained Finland the international goodwill to provide support against the hostile invasion. (SA-kuva)

It has been estimated that, in general, the impact of these bombings had no real effect on the war effort of the Finns, being principally of harassment nature and only occasionally of real significance. One reason for the poor results was the vast and scarcely-populated country, with targets being very hard to find, especially in the snow-covered terrain. Soviet bombing accuracy also left much to be desired, while the thick snow cover often decreased the impact of the bombs. And wherever Finnish (or Swedish) fighters were encountered, it was not unusual for the bombers to release their bombs and escape. The operations conducted on the coastline by the Baltic Fleet air forces, in particular, are considered to have been much less significant than originally estimated.

CONCLUSION

Peace

By 12 March the Finnish military headquarters had informed the government that the front could hardly hold more than a week and that losses would become unbearable. Moscow threatened to tighten the peace terms if the signing of the treaty was delayed. In this compelling situation, the Finnish parliament authorized Prime Minister Risto Ryti to sign the peace agreement. The one-sided peace treaty dictated by the Soviet Union was signed at Moscow on the evening of 12 March 1940, with the fighting to end the next day at 1100hrs Finnish time.

From the Soviet point of view, they were willing to agree to peace mainly for two reasons. Firstly, the resistance of the Finnish armed forces was far beyond their estimates and the continuation of the war threatened to become a prestige issue. Secondly, the Soviet Union did not want Britain or France to join the conflict on the Finnish side. Both nations had made big promises, even including sending large numbers of troops to Finland. Of course, this was a largely hypothetical threat; in practice, moving a half-million-man army was unrealistic, but the flow of aircraft had been going on for several weeks and more kept coming.

From the Finnish perspective, it was believed that resistance could not hold out much longer, a consideration that obviously escaped the Russians. It was also realized that foreign help would remain limited to aircraft and other airborne deliveries, though some naively believed in international troops arriving to assist them. Accepting the severe terms of peace would save most of the country and preserve Finland's independence.

There has also been some evidence that Germany, which was officially neutral throughout the conflict, had secretly recommended that the Finnish government accept the harsh terms of peace, on the premise that all lost territory would soon be taken back and much more. The German invasion of Denmark and Norway was only four weeks away, and its plans for the invasion of the Soviet Union were not far in the future.

Blenheim BL-138 of 1/LLv 42 bellied early at take-off from Juva on 7 March 1940, when the American volunteer pilot, 1Lt Charles Doran unintentionally drew the landing gear in. The bomber was repaired in the unit and it took exactly one month, by which time the war was over. (Finnish Air Force)

Ultimately, 105 days of hard battle were behind Finland. The war had demanded enormous effort and inflicted heavy casualties. Finnish losses including civilians were 27,000 killed and 43,000 wounded. The extremely severe terms of peace were dictated in Moscow, overshadowing the feeling of relief brought on by the end of fighting. Finnish flags were lowered to half-mast, the mood was sombre, and some cried openly on the streets when the news of the peace and its harsh terms was received.

The whole Karelian Isthmus and Ladoga Karelia were lost, with the city of Viipuri and towns of Sortavala and Käkisalmi, and likewise the outer islands in the Gulf of Finland, Kuusamo and Salla areas, in addition to the western part of Kalastajasaarento by the Arctic Sea. The Hanko peninsula and surrounding waters was rented to the Soviet Union as a military base for 30 years. Practically nobody remained in the surrendered areas, and new homes had to be provided for 420,000 evacuees. The peace terms came as a shock. The peace became commonly known as a forced peace of Moscow.

The Finnish President Kyösti Kallio stated in his speech:

> While our army remained unbeaten to the end, it is impossible to understand for the majority of our people, why the battle was not continued. But those, who are responsible for our army and fate, must estimate the possible outcome of the war. To them it was clear from the first day of the war that we, a 3.5 million nation, cannot fight alone against a country with a population of 184 million.

The losses of the Red Army were enormous during these 105 days. Soldiers killed, wounded or frozen were estimated at 500,000, while over 2,000 tanks and close to 1,000 aircraft were destroyed. The Finns had also taken a large war booty. Arms and equipment were captured from the Russians, far in excess of anything bought or donated from elsewhere.

The Finnish nation had fought bravely with a considerable degree of self-sacrifice, which brought high respect from around the world. With its fight, the tough and tenacious Finland had proven beyond any doubt its right to hold its place among independent nations.

Here, war booty trucks unloaded at Suomussalmi are photographed on 1 January 1940. Two Finnish battalions stopped and defeated the almost 20-times stronger Soviet 44th and 163rd Divisions, and captured most of their equipment intact on the famous Raate road. The amount of captured equipment well exceeded that bought or received from anywhere else during the Winter War. (SA-kuva)

SA-Kuva

Marshal Carl Gustaf Mannerheim stated in his order of the day on 14 March 1940:

You did not want the war, You loved the peace, work and progress, but You were forced to fight, where you have performed enormous heroics, deeds, which will shine for centuries on the pages of history… I have fought on many fronts, but I have never seen warriors equal to You.

Ultimately, peace would prove to be short-lived, with the onset of the Continuation War, fought between Finland and Germany against the Soviet Union, which commenced on 25 June 1941.

FURTHER READING

Primary sources
Finnish National Archives, War Archives Branch, Helsinki
Air Force HQ permanent orders
State Aircraft Factory repair records
Individual aircraft files
Squadron war diaries, operational records and logbooks
Combat, bombing and reconnaissance reports
Personnel files
Central Archive of Ministry of Defence (TsAMO), Podolsk, Russia
Russian State Military Archive (RGVA), Moscow, Russia
Central Naval Archive (TsVMA), Gatchina, Russia

Secondary sources
Geust, Carl-Fredrik, *Red Wings in the Winter War*, MMPbooks/Stratus, Poland: 2020
Juutilainen, Ilmari, *Double Fighter Knight*, Apali, Finland: 1996
Keskinen, Kalevi and Stenman, Kari, *Finnish Air Force 1939–1945*, Squadron/Signal, USA: 1998
Keskinen, Kalevi and Stenman, Kari, *Finnish Air Force History* 1, 4, 5, 7–10 and 17–28, Kari Stenman Publishing, Finland: 2001–2008
Keskinen, Kalevi and Stenman, Kari, *Finnish Air Force History* 2, 3 and 6, Hobby-Kustannus, Finland: 1999–2004
Keskinen, Kalevi and Stenman, Kari, *Finnish Air Force I–VI*, Kari Stenman Publishing, Finland: 2001–2008
Luukkanen, Eino, *Fighter over Finland*, Macdonald, England: 1963
Stenman, Kari, *Air Enthusiast* 23, 46, 50, 66, 88 and 120, Key Publishing, England: 1984–2005
Stenman Kari, *Finnish Aces – Their planes and units 1939–45*, MMPbooks/Stratus, Poland 2022
Stenman, Kari and Keskinen, Kalevi, *Aircraft of the Aces 23 – Finnish Fighter Aces of World War 2*, Osprey Publishing, England: 1998
Stenman, Kari and de Jong, Peter, *Aircraft of the Aces 112 – Fokker D.XXI Aces of World War 2*, Osprey Publishing, England: 2013
Stenman, Kari and Christian-Jacques Ehrengardt, *Aircraft of the Aces 121 – Morane-Saulnier MS. 406 Aces*, Osprey Publishing, England: 2014
Stenman, Kari and Keskinen, Kalevi, *Aviation Elite 4 – Lentolaivue 24*, Osprey Publishing, England: 2001

SELECTED GLOSSARY

ABBREVIATIONS

Finnish units

Er.LLv	Detached Flying Squadron
ISK	Air Fighting School
IVAK	Air Surveillance District Centre
KoeL	Test Flight
LeR	Flying Regiment
LLv	Flying Squadron

Soviet units

AAE	Artillery Fire Control Squadron
AE	Aviation Squadron
AP	Aviation Regiment
BAB	Bomber Aviation Brigade
BAP	Bomber Aviation Regiment
DBAP	Long-range Bomber Aviation Regiment
DRAE	Long-range Reconnaissance Aviation Squadron
IAB	Fighter Aviation Brigade
IAP	Fighter Aviation Regiment
KAO	Army Corps Aviation Detachment
KBF	Red-Banner Baltic Fleet
LBAP	Light Bomber Aviation Regiment
MRAP	Maritime Reconnaissance Aviation Regiment
OAE	Detached Aviation Squadron
OIAE	Detached Fighter Aviation Squadron
ORAE	Detached Reconnaissance Aviation Squadron
RAE	Reconnaissance Aviation Squadron
SAE	Mixed Aviation Squadron
SAP	Mixed Aviation Regiment
SBAB	Fast Bomber Aviation Brigade
SBAP	Fast Bomber Aviation Regiment
TAP	Transport Aviation Regiment
TBAP	Heavy Bomber Aviation Regiment

INDEX